INFINITE INFLUENCE

FOR DETAILS ON TAILORING THIS BOOK FOR YOUR TEAM
AND BULK PRICING, EMAIL HELLO@VANHOOSER.COM.

ALYSON VAN HOOSER

INFINITE
INFLUENCE

CAPTIVATE, CONNECT, & COMPEL
ANYONE, ANYTIME

Published and distributed by:

SOUND WISDOM
P.O. Box 310
Shippensburg, PA 17257-0310
717-530-2122

info@soundwisdom.com

www.soundwisdom.com

ISBN 13 TP: 978-1-64095-445-8

ISBN 13 eBook: 978-1-64095-446-5

For Worldwide Distribution, Printed in the U.S.A.

1 2 3 4 5 6 7 8 / 27 26 25 24 23

To the one I'll forever be most deeply connected with on this earth, my husband, Joe. I am endlessly thankful for your leadership and your love. You make dreams come true. I love you. Raya. Ahava. Dode.

To Jen, the editor of this book. You empower me. I deeply admire your work and am so appreciative of the opportunity to learn from you and create with you. Together we're working to impact the world, one book at a time.

"YOU HAVE UNENDING POWER TO CREATE AN INFINITE CONNECTION THAT ENDURES A LIFETIME AND BEYOND."

THE PROCESS OF BUILDING <u>INFINITE INFLUENCE</u> WILL HELP YOU <u>CAPTIVATE, CONNECT WITH, AND COMPEL</u> ANYONE AT ANY TIME, AND LONG AFTER YOUR WORK IS COMPLETE YOU WILL HAVE CREATED UNFORGETTABLE, <u>LASTING IMPACT</u> THAT CHANGES PEOPLE'S LIVES AND THE WORLD FOR THE BETTER.

CONTENTS

PREFACE

TOO OFTEN, GOOD PEOPLE with great intentions exhaust themselves and their resources working toward positively influencing people—family, friends, employees, decision-makers, customers, community members, and more—and sadly, ultimately they never gain ground. They expend inordinate amounts of time and energy (emotional and otherwise) trying to change people's attitudes, beliefs, and/or actions, but find themselves frustrated by their short-lived or lackluster results and confused by the source of genuine, sustainable influence. The good news is, what has seemed to be an ever-elusive driving force behind human connection is, in all reality, simply an improved focus.

From this moment forward, you must change the way you see the people with whom you interact. I urge you to recognize that everything a person wants, says, and does is fueled by their desire to fulfill a need. If you want to influence someone, you must serve their needs. If you want to *Infinitely Influence* someone, you have to think like them and understand their paramount need. The challenge is that most people operate based on their own understanding in life, and they lack the ability to think like someone who has different experiences and needs than them. Seeing people in terms of the needs *they* are trying to fulfill is the perspective shift that will gain you endless opportunity to connect with people. When you master this mindset, you gift yourself an unfailing compass that points to what you must do—exactly which human need you must serve—in order to build Infinite Influence with someone.

Is this easy? No. It's work! But if you've ever felt burned out or as if you've lost your passion, this book shows you what to do to make the work worth it—for you and for them. It gives you a different paradigm for attracting, engaging, and inspiring people to move forward for their good and for yours—a paradigm based not on fear, fraud, or force, or any other one-way, top-down motivator, but rather a driver that refines the thoughts and actions of both the influencer and the influenced—*empathy*.

Yes, empathy—that so-called "soft skill" that often gets lumped together with emotional intelligence and never unpacked to discern its true, integral role in forging connections that inspire personal, team, and organizational success.

Many people desire influence, but few understand exactly how to achieve it. High-level empathy closes the gap. Empathy is the skill that helps you understand and define a person's needs you must meet if you want to influence them. Without empathy, influence isn't gained strategically. Instead, it's achieved only through nonreplicable luck. However, for those who master the skill of empathy, just as when someone goes from simply drawing to becoming an artist, there is a high level of intentionality, capability, and predictable success that accompanies this shift.

Being strategically empathetic empowers you to create an incalculable connection resulting in transformational influence that lasts forever. Without a doubt, empathy is the foundational force

behind achieving what I term the highest degree of influence—
Infinite Influence.

Infinite Influence forever changes the intrinsic reasoning for how the person being influenced moves forward. It can be achieved over time and even in a single interaction. Either way, you earn a lifetime connection. Infinite Influence is the single most valuable way to interact with people, earn success, and make a positive difference in this world.

This is your chance to transform the way you perceive people so you can identify and seize opportunities to captivate, connect with, and compel anybody at any time. Now is your time to make this crucial perspective shift toward seeing people in terms of their needs. Revolutionize the way you connect, lead, and inspire—not only in business, but in your personal life as well. Building Infinite Influence will maximize your business results, improve your relationships, and usher you into living out your purpose more powerfully than ever. A better future awaits—let's go!

INTRODUCTION

ONE WINTER AFTERNOON, I was sitting on my bed, staring at a letter that had a large red stamp on the front. The faded red stamp read "JAIL MAIL." When my husband, Joe, looked over to see what had caused me to go from laughing to silent, he noticed what I had in my hand and then sat reverently and waited for me to speak first.

For the past hour or so, we had been sifting through a box that for years had collected random items we didn't need, would never want to display, but also didn't want to get rid of—similar to the junk drawer many people have somewhere in their house, except this was a 50-gallon gray Sterlite tote that was buried in the back of a hallway closet. We laughed as we came across high school love notes, old trophies, and dried prom flowers. The letter I read stopped our fun. I don't think I'll ever forget the moment that came next. *It was the very moment that I had clarity about exactly what it is that a person can do to be more successful at work, at home, and in every area of their life in which they interact with other people.*

I read the letter to myself first. With every word, I simultaneously considered what was written and the inmate himself, my father. In a matter of seconds, I felt the recognizable gnawing pain that surges to the surface sometimes when I think about my childhood family. Then, because I could feel my husband looking, thinking, wondering—knowing he would never ask to see it himself—I began reading the letter out loud to him.

I looked up at Joe as I folded the letter back into thirds. With a deep breath and a lump in my throat, I said, "You know, I am not upset at my dad for any of his decisions. I'm not mad about the fact that we were poor growing up because he chose not to work. I'm not upset that he abandoned us all when I was 13. I'm not hurt that my mom left when I was a baby either. Truly! Instead, the pain I feel…is his pain. It always has been."

I opened the letter once more and read the first couple of lines aloud one more time. The letter started with an apology, written in pencil and print: "I'm sorry for everything that has happened…"

I asked Joe rhetorically, "Can you imagine what must have to happen to a person to change how they think; to cause them to make decisions to destroy their life, their family, their friendships, let alone any possibility of a career or a life of their basic needs being met? And can you imagine your life being half over, like my dad's is, and still not finding your way back to where you want to be? I have no words. The regret, the pain, the hopelessness. His story, one that I don't even know the whole truth about, must have incredibly heartbreaking chapters."

I didn't know it at the time, but Joe's response would give me the clarity I had been working to achieve for years. He simply said, "I've never met anyone more empathetic than you, and I love you for it."

I was surprised by his comment. After 16 years together, he had never once told me he thought I was empathetic. I appreciated his comment, honestly. Although admittedly, the sentiment was fleeting on my part. I quickly shifted gears as I folded the two pages of notebook paper, their edges shredded from being ripped out of a spiral notebook. I slipped the letter back in the envelope and put it in the box to keep—right beside the embarrassingly hilarious pictures of Joe and me in the early 2000s with bandanas, lanyards, chokers, and camo shorts. All the more reason to return this box of random keepsakes to its safe, private hiding place.

I didn't think another second about the letter or Joe's comment until I was sitting in the audience of a business conference, reflecting on my work with leaders. I make my living developing leaders through books and training, but especially through speaking at conferences. However, at this conference, the tables were turned. I was in the audience to learn, not waiting to speak. I was there to focus on growing my impact through my business.

We were at the point in the branding workshop where they insisted everyone in the audience dig down into defining the root issue that our business solves for our clients. As I was working through the exercise, I played back hundreds of comments and conversations I've had with entrepreneurs, employees, managers, supervisors, executives, and other leaders in organizations. I kept coming back to my default synopsis of my work: *I help leaders, employees, and customers **connect** with one another.* I have had so many clients tell me that is the heart of the transformative work I've done with them over the years. The word *connect* was so bright in my mind as I sat in that session. However, all that is shiny is not valuable.

I was sitting beside someone I had just recently met at this conference, a man named Dave. I didn't really know Dave at the time; just a few casual words and a handshake were all that we had shared up to this point. I could tell he was far more "seasoned" in the industry than I was. He seemed to breeze through this workshop task.

As he sat beside me, finished with his own work, it was probably glaringly obvious to him that I was stuck. He kindly leaned in and asked, "What are you thinking?" as if I was just sitting there quietly, waiting, begging the universe to send me someone to talk through this with (because I was!). I quickly turned to him, and through a whispered voice so as not to disturb others in the room I shared with him a highlight reel of my background, personally and professionally. And then I told him my thoughts about the word *connect*.

He gave a quick shake of his head to say, "No," leaving me slightly embarrassed. However, it was also confirmation that "connect" wasn't right. My unique way of helping people was something much deeper and more valuable. He paused, looked off to the side for a moment, then looked me in the eye and said, "I think your word is *empathy*." And as soon as he said it—*boom!* My mind flashed to the memory of me and my husband sitting in our bedroom talking about the jail mail I received from my dad. Joe intimately knows me and my work—he's read the client feedback, comments, and testimonials—and in that very moment, his comment to me about my default state of empathy felt prophetic.

From that moment forward, I began studying empathy. Uncovering and understanding the role empathy plays in human connection has provided such clarity into what causes some people to be successful while others aren't. Recognizing the value of empathy in the leadership development training work I do has given both me and attendees a clearer understanding as to why some leadership tactics work and others don't.

It is absolutely invigorating to me that the answer for improved connection and success is empathy, because empathy is simply a skill! Skills can be developed by anyone, at any time, with the right intention, effort, and teacher! So regardless of where you find yourself today, this book is going to help you purposefully use empathy to create a more successful future for you and the people with whom you interact every day.

CREATE LASTING IMPACT

How do you define success today?

I have used the word *success* several times already. It's important to note that there are many different ways people define success.

Maybe you believe that you'll be successful when you have a certain amount of money. Or it's possible that you define success in terms of the quality of the relationships you build in this world. It could be that you define success by the number of choices you have in life. The possibilities are endless. Regardless of how *you* define it, from reflecting on my own experiences and studying the experiences of others I've discovered that success can often be traced back to an empathetic origin, which means that if your goal is success, it's urgent that you start with empathy, the foundation of Infinite Influence, now.

Make no mistake about it, *building Infinite Influence will help you be more effective at leading and partnering with others to attain greater success.* Make today's actions create a better tomorrow. Compound your results. Infinitely grow your opportunities. Employing this strategy may very well increase your bottom line, but more importantly, it will fill your soul.

"Building Infinite Influence will help you be more effective at leading and partnering with others to attain greater success.

By putting in the work to understand people and serve their needs today, you invest your time and energy in a way that pays off infinitely. Building authentic, life-giving relationships today will have compounding effects on your life. Serving people is a huge part of the purpose we all have here on this earth, which is why when we serve today, we wake up tomorrow with more joy, more peace, and an enduring sense of satisfaction.

In case you need to hear this, the value of life is not merely in the money you make but in the quality of relationships you build.

Start building Infinite Influence today so that you can captivate, connect with, and compel others to partner with you in creating lasting impact—the type of sustainable, meaningful success that will transform lives, businesses, and the greater community.

> **The value of life is not merely in the money you make but in the quality of relationships you build.**

PART ONE

THE POWER OF INFINITE INFLUENCE

CHAPTER 1

THE HIGHEST FORM OF INFLUENCE

BUILDING INFINITE INFLUENCE IS NOT FOR EVERYBODY, but if you are determined to be successful in working and living with people, then building Infinite Influence is the next right step in achieving the future of your dreams.

To gain clarity on exactly the best way for you to move forward, you must first understand the nuances that differentiate manipulation, motivation, and influence.

Influence is permission granted from one person to another in which one person impacts the other person's decisions around who they are and what they do. Permission is granted consciously or subconsciously, temporarily or forever.

Influence should never be confused with manipulation or motivation.

In essence, motivation is housed in our soul. On the other hand, manipulation is a negative external force. Manipulation is the use of tactics to goad someone to achieve a particular result.

Manipulation can be used to move someone's hands and feet temporarily, but it doesn't budge a person's steadfast soul. In the end, the soul always wins.

Infinite Influence is more powerful than manipulation. Through the mutually beneficial process of building Infinite Influence, the initiator inspires a positive shift in another person's soul. Infinite Influence focuses on serving the most important needs of people, because when people's needs are being met, they are open to choosing a different motivator that will guide their hands and feet differently, to a better result, forever.

Building Infinite Influence is not an option for achieving success; it's a fundamental requirement, especially in business. I'll give you a quick example.

Losing great employees may be the single greatest competitive threat for companies. And in today's world where it's an employee's market, the risk is higher than ever. The Infinite Influence process is hands down the best way to mitigate the risk. However, either due to ignorance or arrogance, there are good people, well-intentioned managers, solid companies that are hemorrhaging their greatest asset—their best people—which is resulting in a breeding ground for struggle and failure. This doesn't have to be your reality! Make sure that you're not using manipulative tactics or misunderstanding human motivation, and instead start building Infinite Influence; it is the only way to ensure the best outcome possible.

Oftentimes in my line of work of developing leaders, I get the unique advantage of building relationships with people at every level of an organization—from board members to executives to frontline employees and new hires. Through these relationships,

I get a front-row seat to the disconnects between leaders and employees that lead to negative results.

Recently, I was talking with an employee, Tyler, who had just turned in his resignation. People at all levels of the organization were devastated to learn that one of their very best team members had decided to move on—to take his skills, energy, and effort to help someone else, another company, achieve their goals. This undoubtedly created a significant deficiency. Could this loss have been avoided? The answer is absolutely yes.

Leaders in this organization realized that Tyler was a huge asset. They worked to lead him well consistently. If we went back in time, we would have heard these decision-makers say that they had a feeling they could not hold on to Tyler forever. It was a haunting premonition for years. Not too long ago, they had approached Tyler and asked him what he needed from them in order to stay. Tyler's response was simple: he enjoyed his day-to-day job responsibilities; his only struggle was that he needed to feel like he was still growing, accomplishing, and achieving something in his life, not just going through the motions day to day.

I came into this situation after the damage was already done—resignation submitted, new job offer secured, and final decision made. But if we look back at where the leaders went wrong, we can uncover their misstep and learn a better way for us all to move forward.

When the leaders heard from Tyler that he needed to feel like he was achieving something, they immediately filled in the gap for Tyler. Not with Tyler, but for Tyler. They left the conversation and started thinking about achievement from how they knew it. For them, growing and achieving something meant that they were moving up in the organization, that they were taking on more responsibility and decision-making power. They were operating off their own story. And therein lies the mistake too many good people are making. If you want to achieve a certain outcome with someone else, you must correctly understand *their* story—including their paramount need—so you understand how they operate and can make better decisions going forward.

Tyler's motivation for staying at or leaving the company was the need to grow and achieve. Based on the leaders' own interpretation of growth and achievement, only a promotion would satisfy that need, so offering a promotion seemed, to them, like the only option for retaining Tyler.

When they assumed Tyler's request for growth and achievement meant he was looking for a promotion, there was immediate stress because with their current team, there was little to no opportunity for Tyler to move up. The people who held the positions above Tyler were high performers with no intention of going anywhere any time soon. The leaders could have manipulated Tyler into staying longer by making empty promises that a promotion would be coming soon. And if a promotion was what Tyler was after, maybe that would have worked for a while, at least until Tyler found out they were lying.

But here's the kicker—the story of what "growth and achievement" looked like to Tyler was wildly different than the story of what "growth and achievement" meant for those decision-makers.

When I spoke with Tyler, he expressed a feeling of wanting to accomplish something. When I asked him to tell me a story of what that would look like in this season of his life, it was interesting for me to hear his story compared to that of the decision-makers. Two different stories from people on the same team who work incredibly well together.

In his response to my question, Tyler said nonchalantly something along the lines of, "I don't know, Alyson, I mean maybe it would be cool to start running marathons. You train, you get stronger, you win, you get even stronger and faster, you win more, and so on. That would be cool. But that takes time, and I don't have the time to train for that between family and work responsibilities. It would have been cool if I could have been given more freedom in my schedule to train during normal work hours, when the kids were at school and my wife was at work or something."

Isn't that interesting? Two different interpretations of a single motivation—growth and achievement.

Consider the decision-maker—even if they would have offered a promotion to Tyler, would it have kept him on the team longer? Probably not. He didn't define success the way they did.

Because the decision-makers *thought* they could not meet Tyler's need, they sat with their concerns and impending doom until there was no longer time for them to move; instead, their worst fear was realized. Tyler was leaving.

Imagine how different this outcome would have been if those decision-makers would not have operated off their story but instead got to know Tyler's story better, learned to think like him, and uncovered a really simple win-win solution to their challenge.

Without a doubt, those decision-makers would have eagerly given Tyler the flexibility to pursue a successful running hobby. And I bet they would have been happy to offer something to support his training—a running coach, sneakers, etc. That would have been a no-brainer, absolute yes, huge win for everyone.

But they didn't.

If they would have met Tyler's need, they would have been able to influence his decision to stay and continue to go all-in with them.

How many opportunities have you missed because you're operating off your own story, you misinterpret someone's motivation, or you feel pressured to use a manipulative tactic? Building Infinite Influence helps you make sure that never happens again.

Empathy is the foundation for building and achieving Infinite Influence. A lack of empathy, a true understanding of people and the ability to think like them, will rob you of both the human connection and the revenue combination needed to be successful.

Building Infinite Influence is a choice—a choice to be successful. You must get this right if you want to captivate attention, connect deeply with people, compel them to move forward with you, and create a lasting impact together: make sure you never fall into the trap of misusing or confusing influence with manipulation or motivation.

MANIPULATION

Oftentimes when people think of manipulation, they picture an evil dictator or mean-spirited "my way or the highway" type of person. However, I meet good people all the time who are unknowingly using manipulative tactics to achieve a goal. It's why they're not gaining the influence they crave. Could you potentially fall into that category? Don't worry, I'll throw myself under the bus first.

I have four children who are currently ages ten, eight, five, and two. Bedtime is vitally important at our house for a couple of reasons. First, kids need plenty of rest. When my kids are well rested, I know their bodies are healthier, their brains function better, and they have the wherewithal to better regulate their emotions the following day. Second, Mom needs rest. Ha! True, but also, Mom needs more time to work either professionally or on the house.

One day, our electricity randomly flickered off and on in the house. Because of this, all the clocks in the house had to be reset. I had a great idea to set the clocks ahead ten minutes and intentionally did not tell anyone. My thinking was that there might be more of a sense of urgency among the family when we're working to be on time somewhere. Second, I thought it would be great to keep the kids' bedtime at 8:30 but actually get them into bed ten minutes early. That would give me ten extra glorious minutes all to myself! I thought no harm, no foul—what they don't know won't hurt them.

Setting the clocks forward didn't hurt them, at least not until they found out what had been done.

My oldest daughter, Willow, was playing on my phone right up until her bedtime one evening. When the clock in the kitchen hit 8:30 PM, I announced to everyone that it was time for bed. Willow immediately checked the clock on my phone. If she had one more minute until 8:30, she was going to use it to continue playing her game! When Willow checked the time on the phone in her hand, she was surprised to see that the clock on the phone read only 8:20. I watched her look at the phone, look at the wall clock, then look at me. All the while, I was sweating from guilt.

As any kid who wants a later bedtime would do, she began interrogating me at the level of a Harvard Law School grad. Suddenly, there was no way around fessing up to the fact that I had intentionally lied to them, and for a long period of time by now. What a humbling place to be with people you care about.

My intent was not to do harm. However, my intent was to help only myself. To make it worse, I used dishonesty as the tactic to make that happen. For a while after the truth had come out, Willow would check all the clocks when I announced it was bedtime. My manipulative tactic caused her to doubt me. When doubt creeps in, influence fades. My actions hurt the trust we had built in our relationship. Thinking *what she doesn't know won't hurt her* in fact hurt us both. Our relationship was damaged—repairable damage, but damage nonetheless.

If I lay down the law, I never want to be a manipulative person. I want to do good for those around me, especially those with whom I'm closest. You probably feel the same way. In order to avoid the negative ramifications of manipulation, you must understand its intricacies.

Manipulation is often thought of as actions masked in anger and evil, but that's not always true. *Manipulation is a tactic where one person takes action to pursue gain(s)* without regard for the other person's good or the stability of their relationship. Sadly, although I wasn't evil or angry, I still used a manipulative tactic to get what I wanted, all while knowing my goal was opposite of the person with whom I hope to have deep influence.

Manipulation says, "I win; you lose." Manipulation is often deceptive, rarely mutually beneficial, and *if* there are positive results they are likely only to be realized temporarily. Once the manipulator's intentions are discovered by the affected person, the manipulator forfeits any preexisting influence and significantly hinders the ability to positively influence going forward. Manipulation is not a long-term, worthwhile success strategy. Instead, manipulation is a tactic born out of ignorance and directed toward a selfish, sometimes degenerate outcome. Harsh, but true. There is never a good reason to manipulate people. Don't do it. Ever. Simple as that.

MOTIVATION

If you're wanting to build influence, at some point you've probably wondered *how to motivate* someone to think, act, or do something. I'll share with you words I've heard spoken by my father-in-law and business partner, Phillip Van Hooser, who is a five-time author, leadership authority, and Hall of Fame speaker. Phil says, "You can't. I can't. No one can motivate someone to do something they don't want to do." And from my own personal and professional experience, I'll "amen" to that. It's so true. You can't motivate someone to do something they don't want to do. Ultimately, one person cannot motivate another person. You can influence them, but you cannot motivate them.

Remember, manipulation is an external tactic used by one person to affect another. Motivation is different from manipulation and influence altogether. *Motivation is an individual's intrinsic reasoning* for decision-making in satisfying needs and wants. If you want to build influence with someone, it is the person's reasoning that you must work to understand and potentially change. While you can't motivate someone to do something they don't want to do, you can influence the choice someone makes regarding what they are motivated by.

"

When doubt creeps in, influence fades.

When all four of our kids hit one year old, Joe and I worked to make sure they started drinking plenty of water. Up until then, the only liquid they drank on a regular basis was milk. We wanted to establish a good, healthy habit from the start. The struggle was that for one kid, whose name I will not mention, because they had tasted milk and juice, it was as if water was subpar at best for their refined toddler palate. We worked so hard to teach them that drinking water was good for them, a healthy choice. We preached the benefits of improved kidney function, regulated blood pressure, and improved nutrient absorption—all delivered in song form for their little minds. I guess for anyone who knows kids or once was a kid (that's everybody, right?!), it's no surprise that none of those "health benefits" mattered to my kid. Getting more water in their little body was an uphill battle for so long. They simply were not motivated to drink water. Any time someone is begrudgingly doing something they don't want to do, they'll stop as soon as the opportunity arises. This is true of humans in every setting.

It wasn't until one of our kids began struggling with acne that they were motivated to drink more water. Once promised by a doctor that drinking more water would help clear up their skin, water became not just an option, but the premier beverage choice for them. What a transformation in behavior it was!

Our child was not motivated to have healthy organs. (You'd probably be hard-pressed to find any kid who is motivated by that at such a young age!) Our child's reasoning for drinking the water was to eliminate pimples on their face! That's why they drank the water. Some might say that the doctor motivated my child to drink water, but that is not true. The doctor understood my child's motivations and showed them how drinking water would help them achieve that goal.

INFLUENCE

Manipulation is an external tactic used by one person on another with the intent of "I win; you lose."

Motivation is a person's intrinsic reasoning for decision-making.

Influence is permission granted from one person to another to impact their intrinsic reasoning with the intent of "I win; you win."

Influence pursues mutual benefit while accomplishing a desired objective. Through building influence with someone, it is possible to inspire that individual to choose a different motivation. By uncovering the needs of people, you can clearly see how to serve them, communicate with them, lead them, and influence them to choose a motivation—a driving force that causes them to act, think, and move differently going forward. Ultimately, the work of influence means success happens when both people win.

You can influence someone for a moment or a season of life—that's *temporary influence.* Opportunities to build temporary influence are unending. There is so much you can do to build temporary influence with people. For example, in his iconic book *How to Win Friends and Influence People*, Dale Carnegie shows us how a simple smile, a listening ear, being a positive person, and using someone's name are sometimes all it takes for someone to give you permission to affect how they think, feel, and make decisions in the moment.

The impact of temporary influence is often surface-level and the memory and value of the experience generally fades quickly. You may be wondering, "Is temporary influence bad, Alyson?" My answer is "Absolutely not." There is a place for both short- and long-term influence.

However, *if you're not working toward building Infinite Influence with the people you care about the most, your actions may have served someone well without creating an everlasting connection and impact.* This means that the likelihood of you being forgotten and your influence lost over time is pretty high. If you're not working toward Infinite Influence with the people around you, you might be left with your great service, good attitude, nice appearance, honorable gestures, and so on—which make for a good reputation for a bit, potentially positive results in the moment, but popularity, praise, and temporary success likely won't pay the bills forever or fill your soul for a lifetime.

My question to you is, "Do you desire a short-term result or sustainable success with the person you want to influence?"

Something to consider: Temporary influence is most often easy to build quickly, and general approaches often work. For example, if after dinner my restaurant server asks me with a solemn expression, monotone voice, and no eye contact, "Do you want dessert?" as a customer, I am most likely to decide against dessert that day. I don't often order dessert after a meal because I am not hungry and don't need the extra sugar. In order for me to be motivated to buy the dessert, I would need something to happen to awaken an interest inside me. A solemn expression or a monotone voice from my server definitely would not inspire me to make a different decision than that of my no-dessert default.

On the other hand, if the server, with a smile on their face, full eye contact, and rising intonation, asks me at the same time I am ordering my dinner, "Do you want dessert after your meal?" I am more likely to buy the dessert they are trying to sell. The fact that they asked if I wanted dessert when I was still hungry would play

"

There are
degrees of
influence.

in their favor. Additionally, their positive enthusiasm would compel me to say "yes" because I want to reward positivity in an often negatively charged world. Simple communication skills such as timing and a change in your voice and demeanor can help you influence someone's decision-making process in the moment.

Using the latter approach, the server would influence me to buy the dessert. Now, will her effort cause me to be motivated to buy the dessert every time I visit the restaurant from now on? No. The influence they built with me is temporary. It is not bad, just temporary. And every time I come back to that restaurant, the server must work to build this influence again. Doable, although exhausting.

If you're looking for the most impactful and efficient way to build influence with someone—not simply to obtain temporary results, but to make an intentional effort once and earn the same positive results from now on—you must serve a deeper need. Your efforts must be more customized than surface-level, general approaches, because you are trying to shift their motivation for the long term. Does this mean more work? Possibly. Although, let's not forget the mutual benefit of working to serve the deep-rooted needs of another person—it benefits both you and them.

You may be wondering—*what exactly is the Infinite Influence I'm urging you to build?*

Infinite Influence is the highest degree of influence. The process of building Infinite Influence is not merely a checklist of smiles, handshakes, and good vibes. Instead, *this work changes the intrinsic reasoning for how someone moves forward.* To achieve the highest level of influence, you must know that a one-size-fits-all action plan won't get you very far on the path toward the goal. The efforts geared toward building Infinite Influence oftentimes become deep-rooted connections and core memories that shape and shift a person's decision-making forever.

Imagine the example of the server who was offering dessert just a bit ago. What if during the time at her table, the server worked to gain Infinite Influence with her customers? The result of her work could be incredible!

I waited tables at a locally owned Italian restaurant in a small town all through high school and college. As an example of the impact of building Infinite Influence versus that of temporary influence, I'll play out an experience that often occurred in the restaurant at which I worked.

Let's say I was at dinner with my friend Holly. Our server knows her tip is largely based off how big her customer's order is, so from the beginning she is thinking about how to get us to order more food and drinks. She works to be friendly with us and provide what she considers to be great service. From the very first visit to our table, she attempts to get to know us. She asks lots of questions, rather than the normal passing conversation most servers use. She focuses on learning about us: why we're here, if we've been here before, if we intend to come again, if we've had any exceptionally memorable experiences here, etc. She asks about our families and our hometowns. The server listens, takes her time, responds genuinely to us, and doesn't rush the conversation.

At one point in the conversation, Holly starts talking with the server and me about growing up in this town and coming here, to this very restaurant, with her grandmother all the time. Holly's grandmother had recently passed away so it was a bittersweet moment. Interestingly enough, Holly's grandmother was a long-time customer of the restaurant, and our server had waited on her numerous times over the decades. The server knew her well! She remembered that Holly's grandmother, without fail, always ordered dessert after her preferred chicken croissant dish.

The waitress finishes serving us our food and right as we're finishing up, when normally we would have received the check, the server comes over and says this to Holly: "You mentioned that you used to come here with your grandmother. Again, I am so sorry for your loss. She was a wonderful, vibrant woman. I always enjoyed waiting on her. One thing I loved about your grandmother was that she always made time to enjoy the little things. Every time your grandmother was here, she would order a slice of cheesecake for dessert after her meal. She loved dessert! Would you like to celebrate and remember her right now, here in a place she loved to be, and have some cheesecake in her honor? On the house, of course."

Holly and I are both blown away at this point. How sweet of our server to think of such a kind gesture! Holly looks at me with tears in her eyes, and then looks back at the server and says, "Yes, that would be wonderful."

From that night on, without fail, just as her grandmother did, Holly orders cheesecake after dinner at that restaurant. Every time she eats that cheesecake in that restaurant, she has a moment of joy, remembering her loved one.

In just one moment, the server created Infinite Influence—a deep-rooted connection and core memory that shaped and shifted Holly's decision-making forever. The server may never even have to ask Holly again if she wants dessert; she might just automatically order it at the same time she orders her meal!

Imagine how much profit could be made for businesses if more servers built Infinite Influence with customers. Yes, on the first night the restaurant paid for the cheesecake. That probably cost the restaurant $5.00 or so. However, if from then on Holly orders one piece of cheesecake every time she dines at that restaurant—perhaps an average of 6 times a year for the next 35 years—at $2.00 net profit, the restaurant has made $420.00 (minus the $5.00 for the first piece of cheesecake on the house) off only one customer because of one action by one server. Imagine the exponential growth opportunity there!

Now, forget the dessert and the restaurant! Imagine the payoff for both parties if you started intentionally creating Infinite Influence with the people you encounter every day. The thought of the opportunity out there just waiting to be realized gets me excited for *you!* And even more importantly when it comes to building Infinite Influence, think of all the hours of positive human moments that could be made in the world, just like the moments Holly will get to experience remembering her grandmother for years to come, if we all worked to build Infinite Influence by serving others—not necessarily to buy more of something for our benefit, but with the intention of being the heart in a tough world.

So while there are degrees of influence, Infinite Influence is the highest, most worthwhile level of influence, and it will be the focus of the book from here on out. You can create Infinite Influence, and in the pages to come I'll show you how to establish such a lasting, win-win connection that enables you to positively shift people's motivation for the long haul and enjoy the personal and professional wealth that results.

Infinite Influence is built by masterfully thinking like someone else and serving their need of paramount importance.

"Infinite Influence will earn you the largest return on investment for your time and effort.

– Alyson Van Hooser

MAKE NO MISTAKE ABOUT IT, the decision to build Infinite Influence is a decision to increase your responsibility. For those whom you attempt to influence, you are choosing to be a part of their success or failure, their happiness or their frustration. When you have influence with someone, you can potentially impact who they are and how they move forward in life. So proceed with caution. Influence is a responsibility not to be taken lightly or approached apathetically.

The fact that you're at this point in the book means you are at least interested in the idea of positively influencing other people for some reason—whether it be influencing a customer to buy, an employee to stay, a decision-maker to listen, a friend or significant other to mend a relationship, etc. I am going to make an unabashed final statement here *for those who crave impact and long-term success*:

- Don't manipulate people.
- Don't get caught up in work that doesn't earn compounding results.
- Live your life to build and achieve Infinite Influence.

None of that should shock you by now, but it is important to note one last time that you can't motivate someone to do something they don't want to do. Yes, you can manipulate them to do it—for a little while. Sadly, it happens all the time. And if that is the approach you choose, then you are opting for a future of extremely fragile and likely temporary success.

On the other hand, in order to be successful in the moment and the long term, what you can do and should do is work to ethically influence someone. There should be no deceit when it comes to building Infinite Influence. Your approach should be known. Don't be afraid to communicate to someone that you want to help them achieve their goals and intend to work together to achieve shared objectives. Talk with them about what is important to them. Tell them that you want to understand them better so you can serve them better. Uncover what they need from you in order to change their motivation for how they move forward. Make the human connection that ignites a rhythm of decision-making leading to win-win outcomes for both parties.

Infinite Influence is all about correctly serving people's most important needs. Too many people don't get this right. Granted, it's not always easy and it does take both time and intentional focus. However, when you get this work right, you will *change the way you see people forever.* You will *connect deeply* and have an *undeniable influence* and positive *lasting impact* on the people and world around you. The work is worth it!

Ready to change your life and positively impact others? Let's go!

CHAPTER 2

HOW AND WHY INFLUENCE BECOMES INFINITE

THE REQUIRED OBJECT OF ACTION
→ THE PARAMOUNT NEED

AS HUMAN BEINGS, we are all showing up in the world motivated to fulfill our needs every moment of every day. Those needs can range from the need of a paycheck for food and shelter; to feeling like you belong; to leaving a legacy; to making more money to help a family member; to avoiding stress; to making a positive impact; to feeling understood, secure, heard, loved, and so on. There is a need within yourself that you're meeting by reading this very book!

Is there an order to it all?

Yes.

Who determines the order?

The individual. And only the individual.

If you want to *infinitely influence* someone, you must correctly understand the order in which someone has placed their needs.

Some degree of influence is achieved when you serve *a* need of someone.

However, the goal of this book is not to teach you how to achieve *some* degree of influence. The goal is to teach you how to achieve *Infinite Influence*.

Infinite Influence is achieved when you serve *the* need of someone—not *a* need.

The need is a person's "paramount need." Out of all the needs someone has in their life, in a certain situation, or in a particular moment, the paramount need trumps all and must be met by you if you want the opportunity to infinitely influence someone to move forward with you toward a win-win outcome.

Here's where gaining Infinite Influence becomes incredibly challenging.

We all have needs. You may choose to prioritize your needs one way. I may choose to prioritize my needs another way. And someone else may prioritize their needs differently than either of us. Regardless of the reasoning behind the order, there is an order of importance, and you must understand it correctly if you want to clearly see your next right move for building Infinite Influence with someone.

When it comes to connecting with someone for a specific win-win outcome, among all the needs a person is working to satisfy there exists one of paramount importance that acts as the gateway for human connection. This connection will compel someone to allow you to influence them. It is by either serving the paramount need—or not—that you are granted or denied access to moving forward together in a positive direction.

Because human needs are incredibly nuanced, your ability to masterfully empathize with people is not simply an option going forward; it is an urgent requirement for your success in infinitely influencing someone.

Infinite Influence happens when you serve someone's paramount need. When using the term *need*, I have to make sure that we're aligned on its meaning and moving in the same direction before I show you the process for building Infinite Influence.

DIFFERENTIATING HUMAN NEEDS

When I was in college, I was putting on an event with some of my friends at church. This was the first time we were given permission from the elders of the church to put on an event for high school kids. This was our time to prove that we could handle the responsibility and do incredible work with these kids! We were all excited for the opportunity and dead set on making it a huge success. We wanted the kids to leave the event energized and inspired and talk about how amazing it was with their family and friends forever!

My friends and I put our heads together and decided to start off the three-day event with a dance party. The idea was to create good energy from the very beginning. The event was a whole vibe. On the first night, in the huge auditorium of our church, we had the overhead lights down, the stage lit up with colored lights that could spin around the room, fog machines going, music turned all the way up, bass bumping, all kinds of volunteers welcoming people in the doors at 7:00 that Friday night. Each college leader had been assigned a dance to do to get everyone out of their seats, involved, and having fun. We tried to pick songs and dances that everyone would know. Each volunteer had to come to the forefront of the stage when their song was on, the lights would shine on them, and they would kick off the song and dance for everyone.

The first song to kick off the event was the Cha Cha Slide. If you have been to a wedding reception, school dance, or listened to the radio, then you know the Cha Cha Slide. When the song came on, my friend Justin went up to the front and, like a man straight off a dance competition show, did the Cha Cha Slide like a pro. He went low, he clapped, he stepped. Everyone was into it, dancing, laughing, having a good time! This went off just as we all had hoped!

We picked other songs everyone would know—the Y.M.C.A., the Macarena, Teach Me How to Dougie, Cotton Eye Joe. The kids were all into it; they loved it. I think me and my college buddies might have loved it more!

We decided that Mitch would finish the night off and transition us into the next part of the event. Everyone in the church knows Mitch. He has been coming to the church for years. If the door is open, he is there! He is always happy and willing to help. And he is one of the quietest, most soft-spoken, calmest men you will ever meet. We thought it would be really surprising to have him conclude that part of the event. No one would expect it. The kids would be totally game for seeing him step up with high energy. We asked Mitch if he would do the infamous moonwalk, first performed on stage by none other than Michael Jackson. Mitch agreed, giving us a silent thumbs-up to signal that he understood the assignment, and the rest is now history…to be told for generations to come.

When his turn came, the vibe was killer; the energy was so high. Mitch walked to the front of the stage, and the crowd literally went wild! They couldn't believe Mitch was going to dance! Everyone was watching, waiting, ready to pump Mitch up. The chorus from the Michael Jackson song "Billie Jean" faded in. I expected Mitch to start sliding backwards, shifting his weight from one foot to the other, appearing to float on water. However, that is not at all what we witnessed. Instead, Mitch stuck his arms out like a scarecrow. He then started ever so slowly lifting his knees to high heavens and stepping across the stage. The crowd that seconds ago was losing its mind in excitement over Mitch coming to the front of the stage as the Michael Jackson song started up suddenly was standing silent and looking at each other confused. We were just as confused on stage, trying to back him up. Mitch took his time getting across the stage and finally we signaled to the AV team to fade out the song and turn on my mic. Lovingly, we cheered Mitch off the stage and quickly segued into the next part of the night, hoping not to lose the energy we had going moments ago.

A little later that evening, I found a moment to approach Mitch in private and ask him, "What in the world was that move on stage, Mitch? I asked you to do the moonwalk."

He was surprised as to why I was confused. He replied, "I did the moonwalk, Alyson. I held my arms out like I was wearing an astronaut suit and I stepped high as if gravity was lifting me up. I walked on the moon."

And there you have it, friends. I said, "moonwalk" and thought we had a mutual understanding. I thought for sure that we would both be moving in the same direction on stage that night; doubt never entered my mind. However, as often happens when one makes assumptions, we did not connect. We did not achieve the win-win outcome we were after. And I don't want that to be the case for you when I use the word *need*. Your success is too important to risk!

When it comes to using the word *need* in this book, I am referring to what someone requires from you in order to choose a different motivation, prioritize another need, and/or move forward a certain way.

I am not necessarily referring to basic human needs such as food, shelter, water, and so on, as established motivational theory would suggest. Although at some point, you may find that the person you're working to influence has prioritized their needs in a way that lines up exactly with motivational theory. However, for a number of reasons—past trauma, stress, new opportunity, etc.—people don't always operate in the science-based sequential order of human needs. And what someone needs from you in order to allow you to influence them may not be a fundamental human need. You might consider it to be a want, desire, or privilege. Regardless, meeting their paramount need is your gateway to Infinite Influence. Whether meeting their paramount need compels them to immediately go all in with you or if it is the first step in working toward achieving Infinite Influence, you need to serve that need if you want to be successful.

Until someone's paramount need is met, it will always act as a barrier to achieving a mutually beneficial goal. How can it not? It's top of their mind, and people are most motivated to take the action that will serve their paramount need.

Unmet paramount needs are the very reason why people say "no" when they could've said "yes." It's the exact reason why employees quit, customers leave, people don't buy, couples divorce, friendships fade, and so on.

Ultimately, people think and act in a way that serves their need of paramount importance. And you cannot forget that you don't get to pick what that need is! Instead, they do! And if you want to influence them, you can't assume you know what the need is; you must strategically uncover it and intentionally meet it.

When you serve someone's paramount need, you open the door for them to choose a different motivator going forward. When a person's paramount need is met, the order of all their motivation shifts forward a notch. Or potentially, by meeting their paramount need, they're compelled to choose a different motivator altogether that becomes the new need of paramount importance. And because of the work you've done to meet their need, your efforts likely result in them choosing to be more motivated to pursue the win-win objective you initiated, similar to the law of reciprocation.

Serving someone's paramount need may sometimes be simple and easy. Other times, serving someone's paramount need may require significant effort and time. Ultimately, you must have a clear understanding of what you want to achieve together, why you want to achieve it, what unsatisfied need stands in the way of the mutually beneficial goal, and then choose to serve that need in order to cause the other party to move forward with you.

INFINITE INFLUENCE ON A MACRO AND MICRO SCALE

Infinite Influence is built by serving someone's paramount need. This can happen on both a macro and micro scale.

Sara Blakely understood that there were women across the world, potential customers, who wanted to hide their panty lines, hold in their stomach, conceal lumps and bumps, and not wear hose down to their toes. She invented a clothing line that would do just that! Because Sara invented a product that served the paramount need for so many, in 2012 Forbes named her the youngest self-made female billionaire. No doubt there are many women, now loyal Spanx customers, who have prioritized their need to achieve a certain appearance over their need for comfort or frugality. And because the paramount need is met, both parties win.

When you see people in terms of their needs, you unlock opportunity. When you can effectively identify the paramount need, you achieve success!

Maybe you're dreaming of worldwide impact, or maybe you're dreaming of a one-on-one connection. Either way, building Infinite Influence is the most effective strategy for getting there. One of my earliest childhood memories is evidence of that.

One of the many times my dad was in drug and alcohol rehab, I had the opportunity to live with a wonderful family in my hometown—a husband, wife, and two kids who were younger than me at the time. I loved their home, and I loved them. At ten years old or so, I wanted to stay with them for as long as possible.

I vividly remember a single encounter at their house one evening. The mother of the family was preparing dinner for everyone. When her husband walked in the door from work, she asked him to run to the grocery to pick up a loaf of bread for dinner. I remember watching their exchange in the kitchen. I always watch people; I study them. It's key to developing empathy and being able to understand and think like someone else. I studied them because it seemed like their life was great—so different from mine. It seemed like something you would have seen on TV before reality television took over. Husband *and* wife. Father *and* mother. Two happy, healthy kids. I was learning even then just how different life could be for me one day.

As I watched, I could tell the husband was upset. He seemed tired. Aren't we all after a long day of work? When she asked him to go run an errand, he seemed frustrated. "Really? I've already been to the grocery two times this week!" he said. Immediately, red lights flashed in my mind—*Warning, Alyson! He is not happy. This could end badly!* I remember consciously thinking to myself, *He is upset, and I need to understand why.* I didn't want to be kicked out; I loved it there! I wondered if he was upset because he just wanted to rest or because bringing me into their home was costing them too much money in groceries. I needed to understand his story correctly so I could meet his need and earn us both a win-win outcome. Because I wanted to stay in this house, I tried to figure out how to make that happen. Right or wrong, I decided that I wouldn't eat as much. I thought that if I didn't eat as much, then maybe he would get to rest more, not have to spend so much money, and hopefully allow me to stay as long as possible. Did I ever tell them I was doing that? No. They probably would have been shocked and encouraged me to eat all I wanted. They are just good people. What I knew, though, is that I got to stay. I was able to stay the entire time my dad was in rehab. Living there persists in my memories as such a special experience.

Did I intentionally work to follow the Infinite Influence-building process at the time in order to create a win-win outcome? No, obviously not. However, it is one of my first memories of how my instinct to see people in terms of their needs and to work to meet those needs ended up with a positive outcome for all.

Whether you're looking to connect with one person or with billions, prioritizing and focusing on serving the needs of others is an effort that leads to success for you and for them, in business and in life. It's the work that feels worth the effort at the end of it all!

THE CRITICAL ROLE OF EMPATHY

To gain Infinite Influence, empathy must be correctly understood and executed.

Empathy is not merely your option for gaining Infinite Influence—it's the required strategy because it is the skill that helps you uncover the paramount need.

Empathy is a tool, not a toy,

   ...a skill, not a trait,

      ...an art, not a science.

Empathy must be mastered, not frivolously practiced.

Empathy changes the way you see people. It gives you a paradigm for truly connecting with people in a way that transforms their internal motivation. Empathy is the catalyst for achieving Infinite Influence.

Empathy should not be confused with sympathy or compassion.

Sympathy is an emotional reaction of concern, pity, or sorrow for someone else.

Compassion is caring enough about someone else to take action to serve them.

"When it comes to building Infinite Influence, the catalyzing power of empathy lies in your ability to think like someone else.

– Alyson Van Hooser

However, without empathy, there is no certainty that sympathy or compassion will help you gain any degree of influence.

Empathy is defined as the ability to understand and share the feelings of another person. And most people stop there, which restricts their progress toward influence. You must realize that when it comes to building *Infinite Influence*, the catalyzing power of empathy lies in your ability to actually think like someone else. It is because of empathy that your focused effort results in *Infinite Influence*.

When you can think like someone else, you uncover that person's paramount need as well as customized ways to meet it—the necessary action for building Infinite Influence.

For as long as I can remember, I have considered what people need from me in order to create win-win outcomes. And because operating with an empathetic mindset has paid off time and time again, personally and professionally, I'm on a sold-out mission to help you do the same!

Thinking back through the past several years I've spent studying and teaching solutions to both general and specific leadership challenges as my full-time career, I've peeled back the layers on simple and complex issues my clients deal with inside and outside of work. Empathy continues to be the common denominator in the solution for the numerous challenges my clients face, whether it be employee attraction and retention, leading through change, improving communication, navigating conflict and confrontation, connecting deeply, etc.

Examining the true power of empathy to spark influence in personal and professional relationships has provided me with a clearer, firmer foundation as to why the leadership development training I do works so well for my clients. Before, I couldn't always explain why certain techniques worked; I just knew they did. Now I understand the exact *why* behind the *what*. Without a clear understanding of why something works, it is difficult to repeat it and get the same results. By understanding the role of empathy in achieving Infinite Influence, you make your future predictably successful.

As I've continued to work with clients ever since, I've analyzed what most people understand empathy to be and have discovered that, sadly, most people are getting empathy wrong.

When I am polling audiences across industries and around the country, if I ask a blanket question such as, "Who in here considers themselves to be empathetic, at least at an average level?" An overwhelming majority of the audience always raises their hands. *Would you raise yours?*

The challenge I continue to see escalating is that more and more people consider themselves to be empathetic; however, the results of their efforts say otherwise. They spin their wheels feverishly searching for the secret solution to influence, failing to realize it lies within building and honing a skill at which they inaccurately deem themselves as being successful.

Before you pronounce a verdict upon whether or not you have mastered empathy at this point in your life, wouldn't it make sense to ensure you correctly understand the role of empathy in building Infinite Influence?

I'll help you do that.

As humans, we are innately wired to consider our past experiences as we move forward and attempt to make more informed decisions. This instinct carries over into how we think about and treat the people around us. Often, this is the very obstruction of an empathetic focus. Especially as we move through life and through business, our experiences change our thinking. It becomes increasingly difficult to understand people who are not moving exactly along the same path as us. And let us not forget that very few people, if any, walk the same path as you.

Consider this. In American culture, we're taught from a young age "the Golden Rule"—to treat people the way you want to be treated. And while I could not agree more with the goal of that statement, most people get it wrong. Most people do treat others the way they themselves want to be treated—they communicate with them the way they themselves would want to be communicated with, they offer employee benefits that they themselves would want, they create products and services based off what they want or would have wanted at their life stage, and so on. And sometimes that works. However, the real sentiment behind the Golden Rule is not to treat people the exact way *you* want to be treated, but instead it is that you have a certain way you want to be treated, as do other people, so treat them the way *they* want to be treated. Maybe, just maybe, the one who came up with the Golden Rule was telling us to start with empathy all along if we want to truly connect with people and make a positive impact on the world. If you want to obtain Infinite Influence, you must work to set aside your own bias and truly get to know the people around you.

It is rare for someone to take the time to truly get to know the people around them. They think because they have worked together, or have been friends, or have been married for years that they know them, when really they know a lot *about* them. I would say the fact that millions of people across the globe are struggling to figure out how to connect with and influence others speaks to the lack of understanding among people. It is important to note that just because you observe someone and are aware of their thoughts and feelings does not mean you are empathetic. You can see and hear all day and never truly understand—because when most of us are observing others, we are filtering their thoughts and feelings through our own assumptions and experiences.

If you don't understand someone correctly, then you cannot think like them. And if you cannot think like them, then you cannot uncover their needs, especially not their need of paramount importance—the one you must meet in order to influence them. Empathy gives you the answers for how to most effectively make your next move!

You may be wondering by now: *How?!*

How do I start with empathy to uncover a person's paramount need?

I'll show you in the very next chapter.

But first, you have to understand the life-changing power of correctly employing empathy. This is exactly why empathy is not to be toyed with; it is a tool that can create a massive shift in someone's life.

WHERE INFLUENCE BECOMES INFINITE

People are showing up every day in order to fulfill needs, and there is an order to the needs they're working to fulfill. If you hope to positively influence and impact someone, it is critical that you correctly identify their need of paramount importance and start by serving that need first. When you address that paramount need, you enable the person to focus on something else—specifically, the win-win outcome you're after.

I first discovered the impact of serving the *paramount* need first and how it is the precursor to Infinite Influence in school from my third-grade teacher, Ms. Conger. There are no adequate words on this side of heaven for Ms. Conger.

As an educator, Ms. Conger had a critical job to accomplish. Her students needed to learn foundational skills such as multiplication, reading comprehension, and writing, just to name a few. We know that a teacher's success directly correlates with their students' growth throughout the year. This challenge to succeed as an educator is made more difficult by students who are not interested in learning. I was one of those students.

My mother abandoned me when I was just a toddler, so I grew up living with my dad, older brother, and younger sister. My dad is a good man. And he is a man who has struggled with the demon of addiction to drugs and alcohol for my entire life. We lived in an environment marked by poverty, abuse, and neglect, so when it was time for me to go to school—I was relieved! When I was younger, the two needs I was seeking to fulfill at school were, number one, free breakfast and lunch, and number two, safety. Yes, I know—academics should have at least made it on the list of needs that were important to me at the time, but when you're living with the fear—and oftentimes the reality—that your most basic human needs aren't being met, it becomes reasonable for a person to shift their focus from esteem and self-actualization (referring to Maslow's hierarchy of needs) to survival.

When it came to my third-grade year with Ms. Conger, there were a few experiences I came to expect and always looked forward to. First, after getting off the bus at school in the morning, I knew that when I turned to go down the third-grade hallway, Ms. Conger would be standing at her classroom door, the first door on the left. Just her presence made me feel joy! Ms. Conger always looked so beautiful with her bright pink lipstick, rosy cheeks, big white smile, and curly brown hair. Every day I could expect to be greeted with excitement and a loving hug. As I walked into her room to get to my seat, I always enjoyed the smell of her classroom—a fruity scent that I could only attribute to the Starburst candy that sat on her desk. Her classroom felt like a dream. It was clean, safe, and relaxing—something much different from what I often knew at home.

Ms. Conger always made it a point to talk with her students about their life. She seemed genuinely curious about getting to know each person's story outside of the classroom. And the reality may be that she did not do that with everyone, but I remember she did it with me. There could be many reasons Ms. Conger was curious about my story, that is, who I was and what was happening in my life. She could simply have been a woman who saw a child who needed to know someone cared. On the other hand, the possibility exists that Ms. Conger was working to gain influence with me so she could get me to perform better academically—a win–win outcome for us both. If I performed better academically, then she could fulfill her need to succeed. If I became smarter, I would benefit forever from that. Whatever her intention, it wasn't until I stayed after class with her one day—a day when she served my paramount need—that she influenced what motivated me and transformed how and why I showed up at school the rest of that year.

During our quiet, individual work time in class one day, Ms. Conger came to my desk and squatted down beside me so we were eye to eye. With a big smile on her face, she whispered to me, "Alyson, would you like to stay after school with me tomorrow and I will put your hair in sponge rollers so it will be extra special for your school pictures the next day? Would you like that?"

You have to know that this happened way back in the 1990s. Picture day was a huge deal then. Most people didn't even have a cell phone yet, especially not a phone in their pocket with a camera on it. Picture day was a once- or twice-a-year event that would result in a photo that many families would frame and hang in their living room or hallway for the next twenty-plus years. I remember so many kids coming to school looking their best on picture day. I remember new outfits, big bows, curls, the works! However, while picture day was a big deal for some kids, it hadn't ever been a big deal to me up until that point. I wasn't a kid who was going to have a nice outfit like other children. I didn't have a mother to fix my hair or help me practice my best smile. I didn't think a lot about picture day before third grade. I did not need a reason to be disappointed. I'm not sure I even realized it was coming up. But while I wasn't thinking about myself on picture day that year, somebody else was—Ms. Conger.

After realizing what Ms. Conger was offering to me, I immediately thought to myself, *Is this real life? I can't believe that I would get to do this. She's thinking about me.* And of course, like any other excited kid, I didn't even have the words to express my excitement; I just smiled ear to ear and nodded, "Yes." I went home and wrote out a note on a piece of wide-ruled paper from my school notebook. It read, "Alyson is going to stay after school with Ms. Conger." I slid the note in front of my dad on the coffee table and said, "Dad, I need you to sign this." He never asked a question; he just signed it and went about his day. I went to bed that night like a kid on Christmas Eve—excited for the next day!

I arrived at school the following morning and watched the clock hands go around and around for seven and a half hours. As an eight-year-old girl, I was counting down the minutes until everyone else left and it was my turn to have my hair fixed. This was a momentous experience for me! At about 2:45 in the afternoon, the bell rang and all the students left the classroom. I sat in my seat and watched each one pack up their backpacks and lunchboxes. I patiently waited for Ms. Conger to come back into the room. As the last student left, Ms. Conger walked in and headed straight to my desk where I was sitting. She reached out, took my hand, and led me behind her desk, where there were two empty seats—one for her and one for me. Usually, kids sit by the teacher's desk only if they are in trouble. On this day I was not in trouble; I was special.

I sat down in the blue metal chair and watched her intently. She pulled out a hairbrush and multicolored sponge rollers. After brushing the tangles out of my long, strawberry blond hair, she rolled up my hair in those rollers all the way to my scalp. I remember she didn't rush. Instead, she took her time, talking with me as she worked. She did not talk *to* me, *at* me, or *around* me to her coworkers who popped their heads in her room to say, "Hi." Ms. Conger talked *with* me. She was curious about my life, what I liked to do for fun, what I did for holidays, and so on. This was nothing new for her; from day one she was working to get to know her students better. Yet it was new to me. I remember thinking that this is what it must feel like to be cared about, to be loved. It was an experience so unfamiliar to me, but I was realizing even then just how much that could mean to a person.

That night, I lay in bed dreaming about how great my picture might be this year. *Maybe a great yearbook picture would change my life for the better*, I dreamed. The next morning, I was up before everyone else in the house. I sat up in bed and unwound all the rollers in my hair. Once every last roller was out, I ran to the bathroom to get a first glimpse in the mirror. I was hoping to look like Mariah Carey on her best day! As a little girl who had never seen her hair full of curls before, I took one look in the mirror and was shocked. I innocently thought there had never been a more beautiful sight! I was a strawberry blond-headed, freckle-faced little girl with naturally stick-straight, thin hair, but not on picture day this year. My hair was curly and voluminous. I wanted it to be like that forever, or at least until I had my picture taken after lunch. After I had my Herbal Essences commercial moment in the bathroom, I started digging through the cabinet under the bathroom sink looking for some kind of product that would make the curls stay until my photo was taken. I was the oldest female in the house. I had no mother or older sister at home with a cabinet full of hair products. Instead, in my house, when it came to hair, there was my dad and his mullet. Most mullet hairstyles consist of a short cut ("business") in the front and long hair ("party") in the back. Not my dad's mullet, though. My dad's mullet was a party all over. He had frosted tips and would stick it straight up on top. I knew his hair was not standing up on its own. I assumed he had to use something to make his hair stay that way. And to my relief, I found his can of firm-hold mousse under the counter. "Firm hold"—I just knew this would be perfect for my hair that day!

Admittedly, I had no clue what I was doing, and I had no one to ask for help. I figured out how to get the mousse out of the bottle. In case you have never used mousse before, you should know that when you squirt mousse out of the container, it is supposed to puff up like whipped cream or shaving cream. I did not know that at the time. So, when I turned the can over, squirted it out, and it came out as a very thin liquid, I didn't question things one bit! With complete confidence in this idea to make sure my curls lasted, I cupped my hands to get as much mousse as possible into my hands and onto my hair. I worked the liquid into my dry, curly hair from root to tip, ensuring I didn't miss a single spot.

Do you know what happens when you have dry hair and you put an exorbitant amount of wet, firm-hold mousse on it? Imagine the fluffiest cat that just got drenched in the bath. That was me. My hair went from curly and voluminous to sticky and pasted flat to my head. When I turned back to the mirror to do a final check on my hair, I was shocked once again. Up to that point, I had a one-track mind about having the perfect picture in the yearbook. Suddenly, all hope of that was lost. However, I remember not being upset about the lost possibility of a great photo on picture day. Instead, I became anxious about what Ms. Conger would say and do to me when I arrived at school. She had spent her time and money on me and I messed it up. All I knew was that in my house, the smallest, most innocent mistake could be made, and chaos would ensue, e.g., police showing up to separate everyone.

For the entire ride on the bus that morning, twiddling my thumbs and shaking my legs, I worried. We arrived at school. Eight-year-old Alyson took what I considered to be a walk of shame down the hall to Ms. Conger's room. I turned the corner, knowing that

Ms. Conger was going to see something very different than what she expected, unsure of what would happen next. When we made eye contact, I saw her pause. I suppose now I know that she was shocked. I looked very different from what she probably expected to see! After a split second, she threw open her arms, pulled me in, hugged me tight, and said, "Alyson, you look beautiful. You look beautiful." Years later, I know she had to be lying—I have seen the picture to prove it! But in that moment, she made me feel beautiful—and so much more.

Although I was initially so excited about having a great photo on picture day, I never spent another moment thinking about the photo after that day. What I do remember focusing on was my time with Ms. Conger after school that day while she put my hair in rollers. I remember imagining that that must be what it is like to have a mom. That must be what it feels like to be important, to truly matter to someone else. I remember dreaming about having a daughter when I grew up, fixing her hair, and making her feel like I did that day. I remember thinking, *This is what love must be like… and just maybe Ms. Conger might even actually love me.*

Ms. Conger had a job to do—educate students. In order for her to be successful, she needed her students to become more knowledgeable. Up until those couple of days at school, I was showing up to her classroom focused primarily on my chosen paramount need of food and safety, not to learn. At first, Ms. Conger and I were not both focused on a win-win outcome.

As a child, I probably could not have adequately expressed my needs to her even if she had asked me directly. However, Ms. Conger took the steps to get to know me. I'm sure she was privy to information about my family's financial status because I had to turn in paperwork that allowed me to be approved for free breakfast and lunch. She could have easily seen that I had only one parent as an emergency contact in my student records. But Ms. Conger didn't rely on static information, statistics, psychological theory, or science to uncover my paramount need. Instead, she used the most effective approach for correctly uncovering needs: she asked, listened, learned, and analyzed my stories. By making time to get to know my stories, she uncovered my paramount need—to feel like it mattered that I was there, that I was human, that someone cared about me. I thought I was coming to school for free food and safety. However, the paramount need she met was the web through which free food and safety was woven—it was love. It's important to note that many people can't, won't, or don't know how to express their needs effectively. Being able to uncover those needs is very much an art, not a step-by-step scientific process.

Everything Ms. Conger did for me was outside of her job description, no doubt. She took action anyway. By doing so, she freed me to focus on something else. I was initially consumed by food, safety, and love, but once those needs were met, I could move on to thinking and working toward meeting another need. I could dream. She inspired me to choose a different motivation for showing up to class from that day forward.

Yes, all along, as a child, I had a need to learn what she was teaching. Ms. Conger could have been the smartest, most innovative, most entertaining teacher ever to walk this earth, and I still wasn't going to focus on learning because I wasn't intrinsically motivated to do so. I was focused on serving other needs within myself. It wasn't until Ms. Conger met *the* need—not *a* need, *the need, my paramount need*—that she influenced me *to choose for myself* to start showing up to school for different reasons than before. Because she served me in a way that made me feel loved and valued, my paramount need, she created a deep, transformational connection with me—one that will last forever. *She created Infinite Influence.* Suddenly, I saw that life could be different. I remember imagining that this is what it must be like to have a family that loves you, a parent who cares. And if all that goodness was out there potentially for me, I could only imagine the other possibilities! I became focused on a better future for myself. It was a transformative experience!

Because she learned my stories, she was able to think like me, asking and answering the question, "What does Alyson need to have happen in order to move forward differently?" Because she correctly identified my paramount need, her actions became the catalyst for a win-win outcome. By serving such a deep-rooted, paramount need of mine, she enabled me to shift my focus from that need to something else. I then chose to start showing up better for myself. I was motivated to be better for me. But also, she inspired me to be motivated to help her be successful, too. I began focusing on how I could do better in the classroom, how I could learn more so I could create a better life for myself. I also wanted to be more helpful and stay more attentive to show her I appreciated her. I now was focused on being a better version of myself and trying to repay the goodness that was shown to me. I still feel that way today, and I always will—working to be a better version of myself and trying to do good for others in the world. That's the world-changing power of creating Infinite Influence.

INFINITE INFLUENCE HAPPENS HERE:

- When you start with empathy,
- When you get to know someone and develop a true understanding of who they are and what is important to them,
- When you can identify their paramount need and then choose to serve that need first—

The opportunities to influence and impact are endless. And when the paramount need you serve causes someone to change how they are showing up for themselves and for others in the world, it's in those moments that one interaction earns you a lifetime of influence and beyond.

Ms. Conger used empathy. She focused on getting to know me so she could gain a true understanding of who I was and what I needed in order to move forward better. Twenty-five-plus years later, I am still proof that "empathy first" is the strategy that works best in building influence, and now I'm boldly sharing it with the world. Seeking out and listening to the stories of those whom you hope to influence and impact so that you can learn to think like them, so you can uncover their paramount need and then partner with them to fulfill it—that is the key to Infinite Influence.

If you are thinking, *That is easier said than done, Alyson! How am I supposed tease out an individual's paramount need from their story, especially if I have to piece together their story from different interactions and behaviors and not from a verbal narrative?* You are absolutely right. It is not always easy to identify the single most important need that a person must have met before they can show up in the world differently. The next chapter will equip you with the tools and techniques necessary to practice empathy in a way that creates Infinite Influence.

CHAPTER 3

A SIMPLE PROCESS FOR BUILDING INFINITE INFLUENCE

IF YOU WANT TO BUILD INFINITE INFLUENCE with someone, you must E.A.R.N. it.

E.A.R.N.

E—EXAMINE YOUR INTENT

A—ASSESS YOUR AWARENESS OF THEM

R—REFINE YOUR ACTIONS

N—NEVER STOP SERVING

Earning Infinite Influence is simple: you check your heart, tap into theirs, and repeat.

E.A.R.N.

E—EXAMINE YOUR INTENT

A—ASSESS YOUR AWARENESS OF THEM

R—REFINE YOUR ACTIONS

N—NEVER STOP SERVING

The first step toward building Infinite Influence is to check your heart. To do this well, you must make time to ask yourself straight-shooting questions and resolve to be brutally honest with yourself.

> ## ASK YOURSELF:
> ### Whom do I want to infinitely influence?

Identify your person. If you don't, you're essentially inviting confusion and stalling progress with distractions that won't help you move closer to your goal of Infinite Influence.

If it's one person, name them.

If it's a group of people—a team, community, segment of a market, etc.—name and/or describe them. The more clarity and understanding you can give yourself about the type of person with whom you are wanting to gain influence, the better. When you can intricately define those you wish to influence, the critical step of uncovering their needs becomes easier.

> ## ASK YOURSELF:
> ### Why do I want to infinitely influence someone?

Before you take any action, you should make sure that any and all work you do in life is getting you closer to who and where you want to be. If this effort and outcome won't get you closer, don't do it. Simple as that.

With that in mind, the next step is to define your goal for pursuing Infinite Influence.

Acknowledge—even physically write down—what result both parties will realize by Infinite Influence being built.

Without a clear answer to this question, you risk expending your resources (emotional and otherwise) serving people with no clear direction as to why or to what end. If that is your reality, the result will likely never be achieved, the connection will remain fragile, and the distance between you and them will increase as time goes on.

Stop and check your heart, though. Be brutally honest with yourself. This is not the place for grace. Are you wanting to influence someone for popularity or praise? If so, that's rooted in pride, and prideful actions create a breeding ground for failure. If you check your heart and what you find isn't good, it's time to potentially halt the effort altogether or reevaluate your purpose and choose a different motivation going forward.

Remember: Infinite Influence always pursues a win-win outcome for both parties. If your outcome is based on only one person winning, then Infinite Influence will never be achieved. If your goal includes both people getting what they want—perfect! That's exactly the way it should be; and with that at the heart of your work, success becomes nearly guaranteed!

E—EXAMINE YOUR INTENT

Let's be clear, the heart of building Infinite Influence is to create a lasting positive impact on the people around you.

E.A.R.N.

E—EXAMINE YOUR INTENT

A—ASSESS YOUR AWARENESS

R—REFINE YOUR ACTIONS

N—NEVER STOP SERVING

This is where checking your heart and tapping into theirs converge.

Because Infinite Influence requires you to meet the paramount need of someone else, and because needs can differ from person to person, the first step in tapping into someone else's heart is your awareness that their thought processes and motivations may be different than yours are, were, or ever will be.

You must possess an awareness that you live in the same world but your story could be wildly different from theirs. This is the key perspective for building Infinite Influence—understand someone else, be able to think like them, serve their paramount need, and repeat as needed.

Some people may think like you, and others won't. Neither may be right or wrong necessarily, however different they may be. It could be as simple as me and you both eating a dill pickle—maybe you love it, and maybe I hate it. Same pickle, but we both have a different story about the pickle. You want more. I want less. Because you enjoyed the pickle, you're more open to trying other pickles, cucumbers, and the like. Because I didn't enjoy the pickle, I steer clear of anything similar going forward. Same initial experience— two very different stories and motivations going forward.

You cannot operate off your mindset of how you would want someone to serve and interact with you because today's world is so diverse and you might expend your resources serving a wrong need if you do so. Instead, you must truly get to know people so you can understand and think like them. You must connect with them. You must uncover and meet their paramount need. This is exactly where empathy comes into play and why mastering empathy is essential for building Infinite Influence.

STORIES, NOT JUST STATISTICS

Empathy is your ability to understand someone else. The catalyzing power of empathy—what makes it accelerate and deepen the connection and influence you build—is being able to take your understanding of them and use it to then think like them. When you can think like someone else, you can see exactly what need you must meet and how to do it effectively in order to gain Infinite Influence in the end. "Stories, Not Just Statistics" is the future-proof strategy for captivating, connecting, and compelling people to allow you to influence them going forward.

> ## ASK YOURSELF:
> ### Do I know their story?

Our life is made up of stories. To get to know someone, past, present, and future, you can't just read a checklist; you'll understand them and be able to think like them when, and only when, you know their story.

Stories are the secret weapon to uncovering needs, and specifically someone's paramount need.

We operate off our past experiences, our stories. This is why getting to know the raw, real stories from the people around you is critical to creating influence with them. It's in the details of someone's story that you will uncover your next right move!

In a well-intentioned effort to understand the people you wish to influence, it may be tempting to seek out the latest scientific research based on what you know about the person—sex, generation, socio-economic status, educational background, religious background, personality type, motivational theory, organizational position, etc. People do this all the time through reading magazine and news articles, white papers, social media posts, watching a news segment or documentary, etc. There's so much general information out there—correct and incorrect—that it's easy for people to consume and then make accurate or inaccurate assumptions about other people.

The amount of research that has been done to help humans understand one another is astounding. And some of the research is credible and can be incredibly insightful. However, sometimes statistics get in the way of truly understanding the people around us. If you fall into the trap of relying on statistics as your basis for understanding the people around you, you risk creating assumptions and misunderstanding the person you wish to influence altogether.

I know for me, I am someone who came from poverty, have divorced parents who struggle with addiction, and was neglected by my mom early on and by my dad at the age of 13. By all means, statistics would not have predicted that I am a college graduate, business owner, wife, mother of four, former city councilwoman, author, etc. as an adult. However, I am. But if you knew me only in terms of what the research says about someone with my background, then you wouldn't understand me, my needs, and definitely not my paramount need at all. The same can be true for every person with whom you interact—assumptions based on statistics alone can lead you astray. Ask me any day, all day—if you want to understand someone, I will adamantly urge you to rely on stories, not just statistics.

Understanding someone is all about connecting with them—nurturing a mutual feeling of being seen, heard, and respected. Statistics lead to assumptions. Assumptions leave room for uncertainty, an environment where undeniable human connection cannot coexist. Learning statistics about people will never earn you a human connection, but stories will. Exchanging personal stories can elicit a psychological, physiological, emotional response that is profound and unforgettable. Stories are the gift you seek out to connect you with people and unlock answers to how you proceed.

Gaining a true understanding of someone can be best achieved by walking in their shoes, sharing in their exact experience. However, this is often not possible due to restraints on time, location, and the reality of our inability to carbon copy an experience. Therefore, sharing and learning a person's stories is hands down the most practical, actionable tactic for uncovering and pinpointing a person's paramount need. Remember, meeting a person's paramount need is key to freeing them up to focus on another need. By meeting their paramount need, the law of reciprocation says they'll be more likely to be motivated to pursue a mutually beneficial objective with you. Effectively meeting someone's paramount need will earn you the ability to infinitely influence them from that moment forward.

HOW TO GET THE STORY

You might be wondering, "But Alyson, how do I get to know someone's story?"

Great news—you already know how! Yes, it's true!

"If you want to become infinitely influential, stop assuming you understand people based on your experiences and the statistics you've read. Instead, start getting to know their stories.

You've been sharing and getting to know people's stories your whole life. Think about what happens when you hang out with friends or family. At some point, one time or another, have you heard or told a story? Of course you have! You might not have told the story with the intention of gaining a connection or influencing someone, but that changes from this moment forward. From now on, when it comes to someone with whom you want to build Infinite Influence, you will be aware of all the stories being shared around and you'll start analyzing those stories and seeing people in terms of the needs they're working to meet. And by doing so, you'll uncover the endless opportunities you have to connect with people by meeting their paramount need.

Don't make this complicated. It's not, even for beginners. Keep it simple. You're just getting to know people. In return, they'll probably want to get to know you, too. Sharing and learning stories is not a science; it's an art. I would even say it's human nature—we've been storytelling since the beginning of time. Whether it's a story about why we did something a certain way today, who hurt our feelings last week, a favorite memory growing up, and so on, we're all natural-born storytellers. It's in our DNA. It's how people operate. What separates infinite influencers from the masses is that when they hear a story, they're listening with intention—to identify needs, specifically a person's paramount need. Getting the story is not the hard part; identifying the paramount need is.

WHAT STORY DO YOU NEED TO KNOW?

When considering what story you should learn, consider the win-win outcome you want. Start by getting to know a story that relates to the goal in some way. Again, this is an art, not a science.

For example, if your win-win outcome is an employee who is motivated to stay on your team long term, the story you seek out should be relevant to that end. You could initiate a conversation with them and ask them to tell you a story of what life would look like for them to achieve everything they want professionally and personally for the next one, five, ten-plus years.

Every time you hear a story, you then have to take time to look for the need in the story that the person is trying to fulfill. It is there that you will ask questions for further clarity, if needed, in order to help you correctly identify the paramount need and how to serve that need effectively.

Let's take this illustration of employee retention a bit further. When you ask your employee to tell you a story about what a successful future looks like for them, let's assume they happily tell you what their dream life would be. They share their story. You listen to them intently as they reveal that they would be working only four days a week in order to spend more time with family and friends. They talk about retiring early and mention that they want to make a positive impact while they work.

There could be a paramount need revealed in that story! If it's not apparent, you simply must ask questions to gain clarity.

For this specific illustration, when stopping to assess your awareness of them and their paramount need, you might consider:

- If they currently work five days a week right now, because their dream includes a reduction in the number of days they work, this could be the paramount need you must meet to keep them at your organization long term.

- They also mentioned retiring early. The possibility exists that they may be working to figure out a way to maximize their income so they can achieve this goal. This could mean they're open to opportunities outside of your organization in order to meet that need. If they pursued an outside opportunity, your objective of keeping them long term would be lost. This could be their paramount need—they may need more money from the organization in order to stay longer (although in the end, they want to retire early; this may be the action that gains you the most time with them).

- They mentioned wanting to make a positive impact while they work. This could mean they want to make a positive impact directly through their daily tasks or they want to have the time and resources to positively impact the people they work with, or they want to be able to volunteer in the community on company time. The possibilities are endless here.

When you hear someone's story, you must listen for clues—clues about what they want. Follow up on the clues with questions to gain clarity. This employee needs something from you in order to stay at your organization for as long as they are going to be in the workforce. If you want to make that happen, you need to get down to their paramount need. Don't be afraid to be totally open and honest with them. Remember, you're pursuing a win-win outcome.

There is nothing to hide here, no ill intent. Tell them you care about them. Express that you want to help them achieve their goals. Be open about one of your goals being to keep them around as long as possible because you value them so much. It's okay to communicate to them that you want to get to know them and understand what they need from you to make that happen. Your heart and your transparency will create a deeper connection through which influence can be built. Ask them if your thoughts on the above-mentioned possibilities are correct. They may very well say "yes"! Even better, they may say "no" to two of those and "yes" to one! You won't know for sure unless you gain clarity from them. You cannot assume you know; that's just too risky. Make no mistake about it, when you start asking questions about what they've shared with you, they'll feel seen, heard, and valued. A connection will be made on which influence can be built.

Learning and analyzing stories is incredibly nuanced. There is no one-size-fits-all step-by-step approach. It's an art form. Listen and focus on what they want. It's there that you'll begin uncovering the paramount need you must serve. I'll share numerous stories with you in part two of this book so you can see more examples of how to work to identify a person's paramount need.

SHOW AND TELL

Seeking out stories from some people may be easy, while getting other people to tell you stories may be taxing.

If you're having a hard time getting someone to tell you a certain story, or if you're unsure whether someone will be open and honest with you while telling a story, there could be a paramount need for that person to *see how it's done first* or *know that it's safe for them to be vulnerable*. I see that often in the work I do with organizations to establish a strong, cohesive culture and build effective leaders. How do you know if someone's paramount need is to see how it's done first or know that it's safe for them to be vulnerable? Again, don't overcomplicate this process. If you're having trouble getting a story, the red flag is the trouble. *Any time in life when you are working to connect with people and there is difficulty, there is a story to be either told or learned.* You can simply ask them if they want you to answer the question first, observe them and identify where their hesitation starts, or you can move forward with the *show and tell* approach since there's really no harm, no foul.

ASK YOURSELF:
Is there a story I need to tell?

For example, I was just recently with a client of mine in the healthcare industry—a group of supervisors. The topic of the training session I was leading was employee engagement. I was working with them to help them understand what their team *needs* from them in order to respect them as leaders. Remember, when you see people in terms of their needs, you gain clarity into what your next move should be to create win-win outcomes.

One participant spoke up and asked, "I know for one person in particular on my team, it's really important to them that their leader be a hard worker. I've heard them express that sentiment many times since they started working here, and it's even been said about me that they don't think I am. But I am." I noticed his peers nodding their heads in agreement that he is in fact a hard worker. "As their leader, how do I show them specifically that I am a hard worker? That's their need I must meet, because obviously I have not up to this point."

My response was simple: "There's a story you need to learn and maybe even a story you need to tell."

To give further clarification, I'll share with you what I shared with them:

I recommend you adjust this based on your unique situation when you get back on the floor at the hospital, but the next time you're talking with this employee, be upfront about the fact that you want to be a great leader for them and you want to help them be the best they can be and achieve their own goals. That's the ultimate goal, right? And because your goal is a winning outcome for both of you, they're going to be intrigued to listen to what comes next from you.

Acknowledge that you all have had past conversations about how important it is to them for them to work for a leader they consider to be a hard worker. Ask them to tell you a story about what that looks like on a daily basis. Maybe in the story they tell you, they indicate wanting to see you visibly working throughout the day. Or maybe they don't want to feel like you're passing off meaningless tasks to them. It's possible they don't want to see you sitting down behind a desk while everyone else is scurrying around. Either way, there are some needs there you can meet: Come around more often for their first response. Or for the second response, you can communicate the importance of the tasks better or stop being lazy. For the third response, you might communicate exactly what you're working on when you go to sit down or make sure you offer help to anyone who needs it before you sit to rest.

Whichever is applicable for you! Ha! You may not always like meeting the paramount need someone has, but you have to keep your eye on the goal—Infinite Influence. Achieving Infinite Influence is far more meaningful than giving up temporary convenience.

But what if you ask for a story and he is unsure of how to answer that question? Try telling a story first (i.e., show and tell). Tell your team member a story about either a really hard-working leader you worked with before or a really lazy leader you worked with before. If you go that route, I'd bet they would immediately have a story come to mind that they could tell you. By hearing your story, they remember one of their own. That happens all the time. For example, if I tell you a funny story about my kid, you might remember something funny your kid did and in return share that with me!

But again, learning and sharing stories is an art form, not a science. You also have the option to tell a story about where or from whom you learned your work ethic. That may be the one that gets them talking! They may tell you they learned to work hard from their dad on the farm. That story may give you direct insight into how their dad showed he was working hard and maybe you could try something similar.

You could even tell a story about a day in the life of someone who does your job. Maybe they don't really even know what you do, and it could be an eye-opening experience for them. Start with stories if you want to understand your team better. If the one story doesn't work, don't be afraid to try again with another one.

As I have worked to share some of my own stories to illustrate points to help people be more successful, it has often been hard to work through the emotions that some stories bring up. It has been challenging to be so vulnerable. However, I have realized that when I tell my stories, other people are compelled to tell me theirs. And the more open I am,

"Sharing your story with someone can captivate their attention, connect you deeply, and compel them to tell you theirs.

the more open they are with me, even if I have never met them before! When two people come together with their guards down and hearts open to help one another, a beautiful human connection is established, and there is where Infinite Influence can be built.

Where there is a disconnect, there is an opportunity for a story to be told and/or learned. The most important factor is that you're increasing your awareness about the person by intentionally listening for what was good, what was bad, what they liked, what they didn't, what they want, how they want it, etc.—their preferences, their needs! You're not listening casually, but intently, to get to know them deeply and uncover both their paramount need and how to serve it. And when you not only listen but also make someone feel heard, connection begins there. They feel more valued instantly!

A—ASSESS YOUR AWARENESS OF THEM

Is there a story I need to learn or tell in order to be aware of how they think?

E.A.R.N.

E—EXAMINE YOUR INTENT

A—ASSESS YOUR AWARENESS OF THEM

R—REFINE YOUR ACTIONS

N—NEVER STOP SERVING

"Where there is a disconnect, there is an opportunity for a story to be told and/or learned.

Your actions must serve their paramount need in the way they require it to be served in order to be satisfied. Serving people the way you want to be served is not always the best approach because they may need to be served differently if you want to connect with them. As you move forward to serve their paramount need, it is critical that you refine your actions to satisfy the need.

Let's say in step two of the building Infinite Influence process, you uncovered that someone has the paramount need to feel heard and valued, as if their thoughts and opinions matter. Let's say that from that moment forward, you made sure you could repeat every word they said to you. You thought that if you listened intently, then they would see how much you value them. And you did it! Every time they talked, you could walk away from the conversation and repeat every word they said. But you noticed over time that what you thought was their paramount need—the need that you've consequently been serving—is no longer motivating them to pursue the win-win outcome you envisioned. Instead, it almost seems as if there is increasing distance between you.

You might be tempted to think you incorrectly identified their paramount need. That could be the case. However, what if you have the paramount need correctly identified; it's just your actions that need refining in order to be effective?

What if every time this person came to talk with you, you heard every word but your physical actions did not make them feel heard? You checked your watch, broke eye contact, looked at someone else behind them, or maybe you're listening while you're walking or typing and it appears to them that you're not really focused on them but instead are focused on where you're going and what you're doing. It could be that you are listening, but your actions are not

"Your actions must serve THEIR PARAMOUNT NEED in the way THEY REQUIRE it to be served in order to be satisfied.

meeting their paramount need to feel heard. Whether or not you are listening, you're not making them feel heard.

If you want to build Infinite Influence, always intentionally work to refine your actions in order to be most effective at satisfying their paramount need. That's where the connection happens—when your actions satisfy their need.

The person might have a need for you to hear what they're telling you. However, their paramount need is to be valued. When you serve the paramount need, you see the progress toward deeper connection on which Infinite Influence can be built.

> ## ASK YOURSELF:
> ### Am I certain I have correctly uncovered their paramount need?

If your answer is "yes," maybe you even confirm that with the person. If your answer is "no," the next best move is to ask for a story again.

If the person's paramount need is to be heard, ask them to tell you a story about what that looks like.

My husband would tell you that in order for him to feel heard by me, I cannot interrupt or interject my thoughts until he is finished. He wants to finish his thoughts and then have me share mine once he is totally finished.

What is interesting about that is when I am interrupted, I feel like the other person is engaged in the conversation, not zoned out.

Two different people. Same action, different interpretations, different stories. Both people want to feel heard. In order to meet that need, it takes two different actions. For those you wish to influence, you must get to know their story so you know exactly how to serve them.

Ask them: "How can I better [serve your paramount need]?" Below are some examples since this question can vary incredibly from person to person, situation to situation.

- **EX.** How can I make you feel special on your birthday?
- **EX.** How can I make sure that you know I respect you?
- **EX.** What would be the best way for me to help relieve your stress?

HOW STORIES ALLOW YOU TO REFINE YOUR ACTIONS

A client recently shared with me a problem they were having with one of their employees.

A great employee, Ben, had suddenly become actively disengaged from the team, no longer wanting to offer input like he normally did or hang out afterhours like he had done for years. The leader told me exactly when this problem started.

The office had closed while the entire team went out for a team lunch one day. After lunch, the leader ordered dessert for everyone at the table who raised their hand to say they wanted it. About half the group raised their hand for dessert. Overall, the outing with the team seemed to go well as far as the leader could tell. That was until one of the managers told the leader later that afternoon that one employee, Ben, was upset at him.

The leader waited to see for himself if he thought Ben was actually upset about something. Sometimes hearing a story from a third party can lead to inaccurate assumptions. However, in this case, the results spoke for themselves. One week later, Ben was indeed remaining quiet and seeming more disengaged. It was obvious to everyone that he was upset.

The leader was told by the manager that Ben raised his hand for dessert at lunch last week but that none was ordered for him. The leader was now fuming, angry that an adult would get so torn up over a simple dessert. After all, the leader did not intend to leave Ben out when it came to ordering dessert; it was a mistake and shouldn't have been a big deal! As far as the leader was concerned, if that had happened to him, he would have shrugged it off and moved on. Because the employee did not handle the situation as the leader thought he should, the leader was upset.

Remember, we all have different stories, and it's our past stories that shape how we show up, perceive our experiences, and move forward in our lives.

The leader's first thought was to go get the employee dessert and bring it to him. He thought that Ben wanted dessert, didn't get it, so he would get it for him. If the leader went to make amends with the employee and brought him a big dessert in an effort to show that he did remember Ben and didn't skip over him on purpose, that action might create a temporary moment of happiness on the end of the employee. However, feelings fade. Instead, the best next step is to get to know the employee's story so you can think like them and refine your actions to satisfy their paramount need. Doing so will earn you Infinite Influence, not temporary results.

I urged the leader to go to the employee and be vulnerable: *Share your story first. Share that you're worried you may have made a mistake at lunch and that you're afraid you may have hurt the employee. This vulnerability right off the bat will likely compel the employee to be open and honest in return with you. If they're initially flippant about the situation and try to act as though it's not a big deal when their attitude all week says otherwise, it may be time for you to tell another story. Maybe you have a story about a time a former leader of yours forgot you or left you out. You could share about how that made you feel and potentially communicate that you never want anyone else to feel that way. If you have that story, you may be embarrassed to be so vulnerable. Don't forget that sharing your story can sometimes be both beautiful and brutal. It is often the bittersweet price of admission to mutual transparency.*

Imagine the surprise of the leader when Ben suddenly goes from apathetic to empathetic. He understands the leader and the leader's intent better because the leader shared his story. In return, Ben tells his story about sitting at lunch the other day, raising his hand to order dessert, but never receiving anything. Ben is nervous to go deeper, but the leader has shared outright with him that he genuinely wants to get to know his team so he can serve them well. With that understanding and no fear of a hidden agenda, Ben shares that growing up, he was always ignored in his house. He was the overlooked little brother to a football star older brother. He often felt invisible and underappreciated. And he admits that now, if that happens as an adult, it's instantly infuriating, zero to a hundred in a split second, for him. Ben says he just wants to work somewhere with people who truly appreciate him.

If the leader would have come at Ben with a huge dessert as an "I'm sorry" gift and not spent time getting to know Ben's story, that action—which didn't serve his paramount need at all—would eventually be added to the list of reasons why Ben might quit and leave, or maybe even worse, quit and stay. Instead, after hearing Ben's story, the leader can now identify Ben's need that he must serve—the paramount need standing in the way of their connection and win-win outcome—which is Ben's desire to feel seen and appreciated, if he wants Ben to choose to be motivated to show up again as an active, engaged part of the team.

Think about Ben's story about being invisible and underappreciated. Can you now effectively think like Ben and understand how being at lunch with the team, raising his hand, being overlooked, and then not getting the dessert he wanted while others were enjoying theirs would make him feel invisible and unappreciated, whether or not it was the leader's intent? Mistakes and disconnects are going to happen, but empathy and storytelling are the keys to help you maintain and grow the influence you have with someone.

Now I want you to pause for just a second. Consider the results you've had in the past when it comes to understanding and influencing others. Do you like the result of your work? Are you making the impact you want? If not, it likely is due to a lack of empathy. But I have great news! If you're not getting the results you want, there is probably a story you need to learn about someone—or perhaps a story you need to tell someone. You need mutual understanding. Empathy is the skill that gets you there. The more you practice it through storytelling and story sharing, the more effective you will become at influencing and impacting others. The more you practice identifying the need in the story that you should serve, the more instinctual it will become. You're about to read several stories, several situations, where the Infinite Influence strategy has been implemented. Seek the story, identify the need, serve the need, reap the reward, repeat. This is Infinite Influence. Your skill building starts in just a few flips of these pages!

R—REFINE YOUR ACTIONS

Serve people the way they want to be served.

E. A. R. N.

E—EXAMINE YOUR INTENT

A—ASSESS YOUR AWARENESS OF THEM

R—REFINE YOUR ACTIONS

N—NEVER STOP SERVING

At the beginning of this book, I said that the process of building Infinite Influence should shift the way you perceive and interact with people forever. It is not a one-and-done activity; it is as much a mindset as it is a method for influencing and impacting others.

That's because change is constant and the needs of human beings are continuously shifting. Infinite Influence can sometimes be built in a way in which, regardless of the change that happens in life, your level of influence with a person remains the same. However, unless the paramount need you're meeting is deeply rooted in the fundamental nature of who they are and why they do what they do, in order to ensure your influence with them continues to remain at a high level you must constantly be aware of their ever-changing needs. You have to choose, consciously and consistently, an empathetic mindset, one that seeks always to understand and think like someone else. You must check in, follow up, and follow through. If you never stop seeing people in terms of the needs they have and striving to meet their paramount need, then the actions you take will earn you influence time and time again—today, tomorrow, and forever. That's the lasting power of the simple process of building Infinite Influence!

Who is on your mind today that maybe you should follow up with and reconnect? It could be that time has passed, needs have potentially changed, and in order for you to maintain or grow your influence you must begin interacting with that person differently. You won't know how to best move forward unless you get to know their story, how life is going, or how it has changed since you last spoke. Focusing your efforts and giving your time is an act of service in and of itself, and it's a necessary step in the unending process of earning Infinite Influence. Building Infinite Influence always starts with you—own that.

If you want to build Infinite Influence with someone, you must E.A.R.N. it.

E.A.R.N.

E—EXAMINE YOUR INTENT

A—ASSESS YOUR AWARENESS OF THEM

R—REFINE YOUR ACTIONS

N—NEVER STOP SERVING

"Earning infinite influence is simple: you check your heart, tap into theirs, and repeat.

PART TWO

UNCOVER THE INFINITE
INFLUENCE STRATEGY
IN THE REAL WORLD

CHAPTER 4

INFINITELY INFLUENCE CUSTOMERS

CUSTOMERS DO BUSINESS WITH YOU to fulfill their needs. The question is, are you serving the right need that will compel them to come, buy, and stay?

FIND THE WIN/WIN/WIN

My first job after college was to sell three products. Simple enough, right? But the problem I had was that there was no way I could sell enough of two out of the three products and still sleep at night.

I worked at a car rental company. My responsibilities included cleaning cars, checking customers in and out of cars, selling customers insurance and pre-paid fuel, and upselling them on the make and model of their rental. If I was going to be successful, I had to sell and upsell!

As far as cleaning cars and providing great customer service—done. I waited tables for seven years so I knew how to work hard and take care of people.

But the sales...

Oh, the sales...

INSURANCE

When you rent a car, you are given the option to purchase insurance on the vehicle while you have it. It was my job to sell insurance to as many customers as possible.

I had to learn people's stories so that I could figure out whom I could and could not sell the insurance to. I did not want to waste their time or mine.

The company probably would have loved for me to sell the insurance to every single customer. I probably could have used manipulative tactics to do just that. However, that is not who I am. I found that I could justify selling the insurance only to people who either did not have car insurance or had a terrible driving record. For those without car insurance, this was a great option for them to mitigate their risk. For those who have car insurance and have a terrible driving record, purchasing this additional insurance was often a great option for them, too. If they did happen to cause an accident, they did not have to file a claim against their personal insurance. Instead, they used the rental car company's coverage. Having the option not to have a claim on your insurance record is truly worth the expense for some people. For those people, one more claim against their insurance could result in their being dropped from the company altogether.

However, most people have auto insurance already, and often they have additional coverage for rental vehicles through one of their credit cards, so the risk of having an accident was not worth the cost of the insurance.

Because of that, I struggled to sell the insurance to the majority of people. For those who needed the additional insurance, influencing them to buy was easy. On the other hand, there was no way I was going to manipulate someone to buy something they did not need in order to put more money in my pocket. So selling this insurance product was not the basket I was going to put all my eggs in.

UPSELL MAKE AND MODEL

The company wanted me to upsell customers when it came to vehicle make and model.

If you came in and originally reserved a small car, the thought was that I would show you how much more room a full-size car had in comparison. If extra leg room was appealing to you—upsold!

If you were going on a vacation for the weekend, maybe what you would like better than the budget-friendly compact car would be the alluring sports car on the lot to take your vacation fun to the next level—upsold!

Sometimes people were happy to pay for a more expensive vehicle. Sometimes there was no changing someone's mind.

In the beginning, *I was getting in the way of my own success by operating off my own story*, and I was wildly unsuccessful upselling because of it. Could that be true for you at some point?

Part of my story is that I grew up in poverty. If you were working to think like me, you would realize that growing up poor caused me to be frugal in many ways as an adult. When it came to the idea of influencing a customer to spend money on a bigger or flashier vehicle when something cheaper would get them to the same place, it just never made good sense to *me*, so I did not work too hard to make the upselling happen. However, soon I started figuring out that not everyone thinks like me. We all have a story, and life continues to teach me that very few stories are exactly the same. Many customers were happy to buy something I would not consider! They were excited to pay for a bigger, more luxurious vehicle that they saw on the lot. Doing so filled a need they had far beyond money. For some customers, I did not even have to ask them if they wanted to look at bigger, better vehicles! I missed a significant number of sales simply because I was operating off my own story rather than with an empathetic focus. Could you be missing the same opportunity by operating off your own story instead of working to understand their story first and serving them accordingly?

PRE-PAID FUEL

While I was barely getting by on insurance and upselling at this job, when it came to selling pre-paid fuel—honestly, *I killed it*. I had colleagues all over the state calling me to figure out my technique! It got to the point where I was selling pre-paid fuel to almost every customer, and even customers of my coworkers! *How did I do it? I had to E.A.R.N. Here's how.*

I have told this story often in training sessions and pose the following question to the audience: "How many of you have ever rented a car?" Typically, most everyone in the audience raises their hand, and I ask them to keep it up. Then I ask: "How many of you purchase the pre-paid fuel?" Typically, most everyone puts their hand down. The same was true for the rental company when I first started: 9.9 times out of 10, people did not buy the fuel. The manager of the office even kept the gas card under lock and key all day since *no one ever used it*. Once I started asking the manager multiple times a day to unlock the cabinet so I could get the gas card, they started taking notice and asking questions.

I will say to you what I have said to many others: after hearing this story, you might just start buying the gas too!

What I knew is that most people do not buy the gas regardless of how much it was discounted. In an effort to uncover the paramount need of customers—knowing that if I could do that, then I could build a connection to create Infinite Influence—I started asking friends and family whom I knew had rented vehicles before if they purchased the gas. They all said, "No," so I asked why. I needed to know their story! Time and time again, people would tell me something along the lines of, "The company is going to rip me off!"

During the mandatory company sales training I had to complete before I started work, it was explained to me how the pre-paid fuel was a revenue-producing product for the company. I learned that while customers are told they can purchase the full tank of gas at a discounted price and return the vehicle with an empty tank, the majority of customers would forget they could bring it back empty or they would end up not using all the gas. This meant that the customer paid for the gas and then unintentionally gave the company the gas back for free.

I learned why it worked for the business. I needed to sell more pre-paid fuel to benefit the company and be more successful in my position. Additionally, because of an empathetic focus, I learned the customer's stories that uncovered their paramount need: they did not want to be taken advantage of! With that information, I tailored my communication to connect with the customer and ethically influence their future buying decisions. My intent was a win-win outcome. I wanted the company to win, and I wanted the customer to win. If both of them won, in the end, so would I.

I had to address the customer's need right off the bat. Don't wait to address someone's need. Be authentic in caring about what matters most to them first. Your need may be for them to buy. However, Infinite Influence requires you to focus on their needs if you want a successful outcome for all parties. It's important to point out that an out-of-touch salesperson does not compel people to buy; instead, they repel people, causing customers to say "bye-bye." Don't be out of touch with their reality, their story, their paramount need. Seek to uncover it and then meet it. Here's how I did that in this scenario:

Me: Do you buy the discounted fuel?

Customer: (*They are likely immediately resistant because they feel like they are going to be "sold"; however, because there was no sales pitch in there, because I used basic conversational language rather than sales jargon, they cared enough to respond and tell me their story.*) No, I've never bought the discounted gas.

Me: (*Now I must refine my actions, get this right. I must capitalize on empathy—show that I am thinking like them.*) I never used to buy it either! Don't want to get ripped off, right?

Customer: (*Laughingly, although surprised at my candor and the fact that I was right, feeling understood at this point.*) Exactly!

Me: The company does make money from it. (*Now they're intrigued because they feel like they're getting a peek behind the curtain and confirmation of what they've always assumed to be true.*) The company can offer the discounted fuel to customers because so many customers will purchase the discounted fuel and then forget to bring the vehicle back empty. Which means the company does not have refuel the vehicle—they make more money! Crazy, right?!

Customer: *Intrigued and now paying full attention since I pulled the curtain back.*

Me: The only way to take advantage of the discount is to bring it back empty. Most people don't remember that when they're bringing it back in. I've been encouraging people to put a reminder on their calendar so they bring the vehicle back empty. That's what I do! Do you want to do that?

Customer: You know what? Yeah, let's do that. I am going to put a reminder in my phone right now to not fill it back up. (*Then I pull up the screen on the computer and charge the pre-paid full tank of gas to their credit card on file right then and there.*) Whether or not they set the reminder is on them. I told them what to do to get the benefit!

The fact of the matter is, whether they remembered to bring the vehicle back empty or not, when they came back their demeanor was different. We had made an authentic connection when I showed them I could think like them, meet their needs, and create a win-win outcome. For the rest of my time with this company, even if one of my customers purchased the gas and returned it with a full tank, they would come and ask for me directly—because they were comfortable with me. They would kick themselves for forgetting what I said about taking advantage of the discount by bringing the vehicle in on empty, but more importantly, they trusted me from then on. And they told their friends and neighbors. People came in asking for me. They would buy the gas. And also really cool was the fact that they were very receptive to any input I had regarding an upsell or insurance offer. They let me influence their buying decisions. They bought, they came back and bought again, and they told other people who started doing the same. The effect of an authentic, empathy-focused conversation, my friend, is Infinite Influence.

Imagine how much more you could sell if you made time to empathize with customers. Think about the needs you might uncover and the potential for you to move forward better if you got to know their story. Your success starts with you putting them first.

EXAMINE YOUR INTENT

Your success starts with your putting their best interests first.

My intent was for the customer to win, the company to win, and for me to win—WIN/WIN/WIN.

ASSESS YOUR AWARENESS OF THEM

Get to know your customer's story before you work to sell anything.

Through understanding their story, I uncovered their need to not be taken advantage of and make the most of every dollar spent.

REFINE YOUR ACTIONS

Learning people's stories gives you the opportunity to interact with them authentically in a way that captivates their attention, connects you in relationship, and compels them to move forward with you.

I chose a sales approach that compelled them to listen and buy. The same sales and service tactic won't work with everybody, but the Infinite Influence strategy will. Get to know people and refine your actions to meet their unique needs.

NEVER STOP SERVING

The most successful people in sales never stop serving.

Day in and day out, new customers and returning customers, I focused on them. If you never stop learning people's stories and serving their paramount need, they'll win and you'll never lose. You will become infinitely successful.

TRANSFORM THEIR PERSPECTIVE, EARN REPEAT BUSINESS

You have the power to infinitely influence more people to use your services, buy your products, and do it over and over again if you're wise enough to uncover and meet their paramount need.

I was touring a hospital with its CEO, and the whole time we were surveying the campus I was blown away by all they offer. Contrary to what the community believed at the time of my tour, this hospital is, in fact, a useful resource to the people, not a useless, underequipped, so-called "medical center" that rumors around the community indicated it was. Ouch, right?

I had talked with so many people in the community about their view of this hospital, knowing that I would be touring it soon. The reputation that preceded it clouded my judgment, so I was pleasantly surprised by what I discovered on the tour.

As the CEO and I walked around, I listened to him discuss their need to see more patients (i.e., customers) to increase revenue and list all the services they now offered to serve their community well. As I listened to him, I considered their challenging public reputation and their past and current marketing efforts. (My formal education is in Business Marketing and Management.)

Reality and perception could not have been on further ends of the spectrum with this hospital and its market. When I asked the CEO what he thought the overall community perception of the hospital was, he hit the nail on the head; he wasn't oblivious to the fact that their reputation was bad and it was hindering their ability to attract new and return patients. And yet I had just been given a front-row seat to all the incredibly specialized services the hospital offered, which in fact made it *not* the "useless, underequipped, one-stop band-aid shop" that many in the community referred to it as.

If you want to attract and retain customers for life, executing the Infinite Influence process is critical.

This hospital desperately needed to build influence in its community, and they needed to transform their reputation in order to do so. Here's how they revised their approach to do just that.

From research, we knew that community members, potential customers/patients, were choosing to bypass this hospital to drive at least an hour to a different hospital that they felt was more trustworthy because it had the equipment and staff to take care of them and their loved ones. The hospital's market was full of people who had a need to know that when they visited this hospital, they would get the care they desperately needed.

Compare that paramount need of patients with the marketing efforts of the hospital.

Most of the marketing efforts I saw from the hospital advertised to their potential customers/patients their community philanthropy, short ER wait times, and employee recognition of years of service. Their marketing was working to serve needs that were not at the top of their potential patients' list. Patients cared less about what the hospital was giving back to the community and more about what the hospital could do for them when they needed medical attention.

Because that's the story the hospital was telling, the rest of their story—services offered, quality of work, etc.—was being left open to interpretation, which we knew wasn't being interpreted the way the hospital needed/wanted, and the lack of new patients was proof.

"If you want to attract and retain customers for life, executing the Infinite Influence process is critical.

And while the disconnect between the organization and the community was bad for the hospital, it was also bad for the people in the community. There were hurting people driving well out of their way, putting themselves through the agony of a long drive while suffering in pain, enduring the anxiety of uncertainty when it came to getting solutions for their health, all because they didn't believe that the help they needed was right in their backyard.

It's sad to see that when people don't serve the paramount need of others, so much can be lost for so many. In these situations, everyone loses.

The CEO and I had conversations about the community's perspective on the hospital and the challenges it presented from a business standpoint. Referencing those conversations, I asked, "We know the negative perception and stories that community members often share with their friends, family, and neighbors—stories that suggest your hospital is never able to take care of serious ailments. However, let me ask you this question: When someone in the community thinks and talks about your hospital, what do you want that story to be? What need can your hospital really serve for the people in this community?"

He was taken aback. "I hadn't thought of it exactly that way before, in terms of a story and a paramount need."

After a moment, he said, "I want them to tell a story about how they know that we will get them safely to the next right stop, whether it be healed to go home or safely transported to another hospital for more specialized services. I don't want them to ever have a story about not visiting us first and then struggling unnecessarily or unsafely to get to somewhere else for care." And as he finished his own comment, processing the words himself in real time, you could see the *"aha" moment*.

In their marketing efforts, they had been pushing how much philanthropic work they do for community, the quick ER wait times, and the longevity of their staff, but that wasn't meeting the paramount need of most community members. They cared more about the exact services the hospital offered than those other aspects of the hospital. Because of the disconnect, both parties were losing.

Imagine the difference the hospital saw when they started basing their marketing efforts on how they meet the paramount need of their most desirable patient.

Instead of advertising the philanthropic investment they make in the community, they shared a story about how an elderly man with a broken hip didn't have to drive an hour in excruciating pain to be seen by a doctor and instead could be stabilized there, pain minimized, and transported to his provider of choice to help him heal the hip.

Instead of marketing short ER wait times, they shared stories about taking care of an emergency gall bladder removal. The need often wasn't about the wait time, because people were willing to wait while they drove somewhere else. Instead, many people had no clue this hospital could perform such services.

The opportunities to market to your ideal customer's paramount need are endless, just as they were for this hospital. And when organizations start speaking to their customers' paramount needs, they maximize the opportunity to infinitely influence customers to come again and again. Like wildfire, those customers will spread the word so that everyone they know can enjoy the same benefits, too. The opportunity for influence and impact compounds, and it

"When organizations start speaking to their customers' paramount needs, they maximize the opportunity to infinitely influence customers to come again and again.

all starts with empathy—understanding your people and being able to think like them. When you can think like them, you can market to them in a way that captivates their attention, connects with their paramount need, and compels them to do business with you. And when your goal is their good, you have a perfect recipe for massive positive impact. That's the power of the Infinite Influence process.

EXAMINE YOUR INTENT

Infinite Influence requires a win-win outcome.

If the hospital served more people, then fewer people would risk prolonged pain, increased harm, and exacerbated inconvenience driving to out-of-the-way hospitals, *and* the hospital would be more profitable. A winning outcome for all.

ASSESS YOUR AWARENESS OF THEM

To achieve Infinite Influence, you must make sure you understand what someone needs from you in order to change their motivation behind, and approach to, decision-making.

The hospital's community had an inadequate understanding of the benefits and services they offered, and because of that, community members were choosing to bypass it. Once they became aware of their customers' need to know the services the hospital could perform for them, they realized their marketing efforts were not directed toward the right ends.

REFINE YOUR ACTIONS

Humans are captivated by stories they resonate with.

Once the hospital possessed an awareness of their customers' paramount need, it became clear which stories the marketing efforts needed to tell to earn results.

NEVER STOP SERVING

People evolve. To infinitely influence someone, you must always be looking to serve their paramount need. This need may stay the same forever, or it may change. You don't know how to best serve someone unless you continually seek to uncover and serve their paramount need.

For the hospital, this means that as the community grows and evolves, they need to keep a finger on the pulse of the community's changing needs, continually evolving the role they are fulfilling, the services they are offering, and the messaging they are creating about these services.

CHAPTER 5

INFINITELY INFLUENCE TEAM MEMBERS

THE MOST SUCCESSFUL TEAMS will be those that create *leaders* at every level of the organization.

Leaders serve the needs of those to whom they report and those who report to them. On a team, when everyone is working to serve the needs of others in pursuit of a win-win outcome, success becomes inevitable.

In my work as a leadership trainer and consultant, I get the unique advantage of hearing perspectives from people at all levels of organizations. It does take focused work to quickly build authentic relationships with everyone from the CEO to an emerging leader, but it is necessary. The connection we build allows us to have extremely candid conversations. Oftentimes, I get a front-row seat to the disconnect between two people who are on the same team but have ended up working in competing directions. If you want to work better as a team, everyone must work to infinitely influence once another. This strategy is key to leading effectively up and down in an organization.

THINK LIKE THEM BEFORE YOU COMMUNICATE WITH THEM

I was working with the owner of a multi-million-dollar company who was pursuing improved employee engagement, retention, and performance. His team made it known that they wanted to better understand the strategic side of the business—they wanted to know the vision of the business and how their everyday responsibilities contributed to the achievement of the company's big goal. You could say they were seeking purpose. As any good leader would do, the owner made it his mission to share more information with his team, with his intention being to relieve any concerns and provide clarity and purpose to each person. I came in after several failed attempts to achieve this goal, and there was one story in particular that was the perfect example of the integral role empathy plays in facilitating Infinite Influence in the workplace. And if you have ever been in a meeting—or led a meeting—where the organization's numbers were shared, you might just want to listen up.

In one all-employee meeting, the owner decided to share the organization's income statement. He thought that if the employees could actually see the numbers of the business, then they would better understand why certain strategic decisions have been and must be made. With clarity comes unity, so he thought. He walked into the meeting fully anticipating employees to emerge enlightened and enthusiastic about their future as a team. And throughout the entire meeting, everyone said his excitement was palpable as he presented the inaugural behind-the-curtain look at the organization's financials.

"If you want to infinitely influence someone, you must first be able to think like them.

– Alyson Van Hooser

Imagine his surprise and disappointment when he returned to the office the next day and a large portion of the team's response to his message was not excitement and next-level engagement but instead heightened frustration. One employee told him privately that she didn't hear a word he said once he put the income statement up. She saw the salary expense for the company and started trying to figure out where she likely stood compared to everyone else. She said she knows she plays a critical role in the team's success and is someone who always goes above and beyond. However, she was surprised to realize suddenly that her compensation, when compared to her colleagues, did not match her value to the team's success.

Whether the employee is right or wrong, we have a leader who is wanting to influence his team to become more engaged, stay longer, and perform better. And with good intentions, he was doing everything he could think of to make it happen. However, therein lies the problem. He was doing everything *he* could think of. Instead, if you want to influence employees to go all in with you, the best approach is to think like them before you communicate with them. This is incredibly difficult in a diverse world, which is why empathy and getting to know someone's story are not only options for successfully influencing someone—they are fundamental requirements.

Good intentions will not create the connections necessary for Infinite Influence if the actions don't serve the paramount need. Instead of operating with good intentions, operate with strategy— the Infinite Influence strategy. Infinite Influence requires you to uncover the needs of the people with whom you have surrounded yourself and be intentional about meeting them. The Infinite Influence strategy could have earned this CEO the engagement result he craved. Here's how.

"Good intentions will not create the connections necessary for Infinite Influence if the actions don't serve the paramount need.

EXAMINE YOUR INTENT

Leaders who crave Infinite Influence are looking for the company to win, the supervisor to win, and the employee to win.

This CEO's intentions were honorable. But good intentions don't always produce good results. Instead, a future-proof strategy is required—the Infinite Influence strategy, which enables leaders to identify and act on the scenario that is truly a win-win for everyone involved.

ASSESS YOUR AWARENESS OF THEM

Managers must be able to think like employees, and employees must be able to think like their manager.

The most successful organizations will be those that create a culture of prioritizing empathy and building Infinite Influence at every level of the team. When there is mutual understanding, every other aspect of teamwork becomes easier to navigate.

REFINE YOUR ACTIONS

The same stimuli can cause an array of reactions among a group of people on a team. You must choose the action that earns you the result you want.

The decision to share all the information or just some of the information is the difference between success and failure in the CEO's case. All the information was invigorating for the executives on the team. All the information was deflating for many others on the team. To achieve Infinite Influence, you must consistently work to improve your actions to connect with your people.

"Leaders who crave Infinite Influence are looking for the company to win, the supervisor to win, and the employee to win.

NEVER STOP SERVING

Mistakes will be made in the pursuit to achieve Infinite Influence. One of the best moves you can make is being upfront with people about your intent to understand them and help them win. When you do that, you open the door for forgiveness when wrong turns are made on the road to mutual success.

Never leave a mistake unaddressed. Address it head-on and apologize. And never stop showing up and serving your people better next time. The pursuit of Infinite Influence is about consistently seeking to understand and serve people in a way that leads to a mutually beneficial outcome. People will take notice of your effort, and because of the law of reciprocation, they'll likely be even more committed to helping you understand them and working with you for mutual good.

THE TRANSFORMATIONAL POWER OF A SHARED TEAM STORY

A vice president of a very successful start-up company was sitting across the table from me at dinner the night after our first group leadership development session. I was brought in to help the leaders of this company understand exactly how to engage their employees in order to build a stronger team and improve the culture of the organization.

We were in a private room at the restaurant, and everyone was sharing their thoughts from our session earlier in the day. It was the VP's turn to share his reflections. With all eyes on him, he looked at me and asked, "Why don't they care? How do we get our team

"Never stop showing up and serving your people better next time.

to care as much about the work we do and the people we work with, just like the people sitting around this table?" You could hear the desperation in his voice. As soon as he finished talking, all eyes darted toward me, begging to have the magic answer.

You have to know that I had spent hours with these people earlier in the day. For a large portion of the day together, I was focused on learning about them, their executive team specifically. I spent time asking them strategic questions to help me get to know them quickly, understand their background, and establish a foundational perspective of where they've been and where they want to go. Due to those well-placed questions they started sharing their stories with me. So immediately when I was asked this question, I remembered a story they shared with me earlier in the day.

I had been looking at the VP, but I turned to look at Jim and said:

Jim, earlier today you shared a story with me about you and the people in this room. You all ended up chiming in, reminiscing on the days when you all weren't in the corner offices with floor-to-ceiling windows overlooking the city skyline. Instead, your shared story was that you were all sitting inches apart at plastic folding tables, working on really old computers. You all commented about putting in long nights, even weekends and holidays. Then I started looking around the room, making eye contact with all of them. I specifically remember you all saying that you became a family during those first few years as you worked so closely, trying to build the business to where it is today. And that is your story! Your past story fuels your current and future needs. Right now, all of you are wanting, needing the rest of the team to feel and think the way that you do. You're thinking that if they did, the organization would be more successful. And that may be true. Although, we can't lose sight of the fact that you all have a shared story about this company. One that none of the people outside of this room share with you. Instead, their story is likely very different, so they have no reason to feel the same way you do. Many of them came into this organization in its prime, not during the early struggle. They see a tight-knit, high-performing leadership team, a successful organization in a growing market, and an opportunity here for them to make a living. Without a focus on giving them all a shared experience similar to yours, it doesn't make sense to ask, "Why don't they feel about this business and this team the way that I do?" Instead, a better question is, "What story/experience do they need to have that will influence them to shift their motivations, and how and when am I going to make that happen?" It will be after you have uncovered their paramount need that infinitely connects you with them and allows you to influence them to move forward differently.

Because you all have a deep, shared connection. Because you all had a need to build something powerful, make a positive impact, even make a lot of money. Because you all met each other's needs, you will forever be connected. If you want others to feel about the team the way you all feel about one another, you have to start meeting their needs. Are you sure you know what they are? Silence. Shoulder shrugs. Eyes darting to the table. Well, let's start there.

The process of Infinite Influence forges human connections that withstand the test of time and endure the struggles of life. It is with Infinite Influence that teams become selfless and successful.

For any organization wanting their team to be more engaged in creating a successful organization, the Infinite Influence strategy will enable you to uncover the specific tactics that will work for your unique team.

"The process of Infinite Influence forges human connections that withstand the test of time and endure the struggles of life. It is with Infinite Influence that teams become selfless and successful.

EXAMINE YOUR INTENT

Highly engaged teams create highly successful businesses because everyone is all in on doing what it takes to achieve the mutually beneficial goal.

ASSESS YOUR AWARENESS OF THEM

Highly engaged teams understand the unique needs of their team members.

REFINE YOUR ACTIONS

Highly engaged teams know exactly how to communicate and make decisions for and with their teammates in a way that inspires increased loyalty and performance.

NEVER STOP SERVING

Highly engaged teams are the most adept at capitalizing on opportunities in an ever-changing world because they never stop seeking to understand and serve people's paramount need in pursuit of a win-win outcome.

The next time you are frustrated or disappointed with how someone is showing up, whether it be an employee, leader, volunteer, etc., don't try to convince them to do what you want; instead, work to infinitely influence them. Check your heart and then tap into theirs. It's then that you'll free them up to pursue a win-win goal with you.

"Highly engaged teams understand the unique needs of their team members.

ENSURE YOUR INTENT TO HELP NEVER CAUSES HARM

Servant leadership is a popular mindset in today's workforce. Are there outliers who are consumed with themselves, their success, and want everything to be about them? Yes. Although, as someone who has dedicated my life to developing leaders, I hear fewer stories and meet fewer of those people in the workforce every year. That's a great trend, right? Absolutely! However, the challenge is that good works don't earn us Infinite Influence. Good deeds might buy you time and goodwill, but unless you meet the paramount need of another person, you're building only a good reputation, not Infinite Influence. And don't forget, working to build Infinite Influence allows you to impact the way people make decisions on everything from who they are to what they believe and what they will do. Infinite Influence is where leaders transform the trajectory of lives, careers, and businesses!

Sarah, the MVP of the operations department of a bank, walks into her boss's office on a Friday morning to have a conversation she had been preparing and working up the nerve for all week. Her boss, Emily, is more than happy to sit down with her most knowledgeable and highest-performing employee.

After the usual pleasantries, Emily asks Sarah how she can help her this morning.

Emily responds very professionally, laying out all the additional responsibilities and educational opportunities she has taken on over the past six months. The list is quite extensive.

Emily listens carefully and agrees with everything Sarah says.

"Infinite Influence allows you to impact the way people make decisions on everything from who they are to what they believe and what they will do.

Then, Sarah boldly asks for a substantial increase in her salary for the significant increase in value she is bringing to the table.

Immediately, Emily remembers that Sarah was at the low end of the compensation range for her position. Emily makes up her mind that she is going to say "yes" to Sarah, but before she discloses that, she wants to help Sarah. Sarah is about 20 years younger than her, and Emily is very focused on making a positive impact in the lives of those on her team, especially those young enough to be her child. Emily is a good person and truly cares about her people.

Emily responds to Sarah by thanking her for coming to her about this. She is impressed! Emily goes on to talk about how she is not sure if she would have had the same courage when she was Sarah's age.

Sarah can feel the pressure of the meeting start to dissipate. She is relieved and feels she can start to relax.

But then...

Emily goes on to mention the recent home renovation Sarah and her husband completed, how Sarah's two girls always are dressed in the cutest outfits, and how great it must be now to have a brand-new SUV with third-row seating. After all of the compliments, Sarah says, "Emily, as someone who is old enough to be your mother and as someone who has had the pleasure of working with you for years, I want to offer you some words of wisdom: You do not have to 'keep up with the Joneses.' You don't have to have the nicest house, clothes, and cars—especially if it is putting you in a financial bind."

Emily went from relaxed to furious, though she remained totally composed through it all. She smiled and nodded and said, "Thank you." Then Emily told her she would be more than happy to approve her raise and would work to get final approval by the end of next week. Again, Sarah smiled and thanked Emily.

Emily was absolutely shocked when she opened her email on Monday morning and saw Sarah had sent her a message saying she was putting in her two weeks' notice. She could not understand how her best employee who had just asked for a raise—and got it—was now quitting two days later.

I had an opportunity to talk with Sarah before she left the organization. Sarah loved her work, the location of her office, her coworkers, and the possibility of future opportunities at the organization. However, she did not like her boss going where she wasn't invited. Sarah never asked Emily for personal financial tips. As Emily made comments with good intentions, all Sarah heard was criticism and judgment.

Sarah entered Emily's office working toward meeting her need to feel appreciated and respected.

Emily tried to help—some may even say *mentor*—Sarah by offering her an experienced perspective. I can see where that would be a nice gesture if it is what the other person wants.

However, when people come directly to you to meet a need and you don't do it, or don't do it first, you immediately begin forfeiting any existing influence you have with that person. That is a heavy risk to take, because influence is more easily lost than gained.

Sarah told me straight up that life is too short to work with someone who does not appreciate, respect, or trust your decisions; therefore, she was going to go find another leader who would.

Ouch.

Does the possibility exist that you may be doing good work to serve the people around you while also causing issues because you have not spent time truly getting to know your people, uncovering their paramount need, and working to make sure that it is met before you enter into your own agenda? Don't be the reason you fail. Be the cause for never-ending success for you and the people around you! Use the Infinite Influence strategy to captivate attention, connect deeply, compel others to pursue a mutual goal, and create a lasting impact on the people who matter most to you.

EXAMINE YOUR INTENT

Examining your intent is the key *first* step in building Infinite Influence. Once your intent is established, step two will help you understand if your intended impact can be realized based off the needs the other person has.

Emily's intent to help Sarah was honorable. However, step two is critical to understanding the unmet need Sarah had that Emily could or could not fill.

ASSESS YOUR AWARENESS OF THEM

Understanding someone's paramount need will help you avoid trespassing on territory into which you were neither invited nor welcomed. Instead, you'll see exactly where to focus your effort to earn the best outcome.

REFINE YOUR ACTIONS

Uncovering the paramount need you must serve to infinitely influence someone will unlock the exact next step you must take.

This eliminates the possibility of wasting resources, time, attention, money, etc. that will never earn you the result you're after.

NEVER STOP SERVING

Human needs are ever-changing. The successful leaders will be those who consistently seek to understand and empathize with their team members and adapt their actions to serve accordingly.

CHAPTER 6

INFINITELY INFLUENCE FRIENDS AND FAMILY

INTENTIONALLY WORKING to infinitely influence our loved ones may be the most meaningful actions we take in this life.

THE REVOLUTIONARY POWER OF THE DEBRIEF

I started dating my husband when I was 15, a mere two years after I was abandoned by my immediate family. Thinking back, I cannot picture in my mind a time when I sat with my family and had dinner around the table.

However, family dinner around the dining room table was a normal way of life for Joe's family. If I was at their house, Joe's mom, Susan, always invited me to join them, which I so appreciated.

I sat down to dinner one evening with their family, all five of them. Joe's dad, Phil, whom I had not had the opportunity to get to know yet because he traveled frequently for work, was home this evening. As a young teenager in love, of course I was trying

"Intentionally working to infinitely influence our loved ones may be the most meaningful actions we take in this life.

to put my best foot forward—especially because I felt like I was underqualified to be around this family anyway. To me, at 15, they seemed very different from me. I grew up on the poor side of town; they did not. I thought my family was broken; theirs was not. I assumed they had money; I knew I sure didn't.

From previous dinners with the family (minus Phil), I knew they liked to talk. They were big into asking each other questions, especially introspective questions. I really enjoyed this! It was new to me—to see people being so real and kind with one another—and I liked it.

That evening, when the table was set with sweet tea, side salads, and spaghetti, we prayed, dug into our food, and conversation began. After lots of laughs, Phil turned to ask me a question. After all, he and I had hardly talked before. He said, "Alyson, tell me about your family." A simple question. Nothing too deep. Acceptable for a 15-year-old girl.

From a very early age, I have seen the people around me in terms of their needs. I studied what people did and analyzed why they would do it. When my dad was in and out of rehab over the years, I would live with different families. I had so many different people to study. So when Phil asked this question, I started thinking about his need—what he needed from me in order to give his approval to keep dating his son. After all, there was a part of me that felt there was no way I would be lucky enough to be able to date Joe for long anyway; he was way out of my league on so many levels.

I paused, and in a matter of seconds I came to the internal conclusion that Phil knew my family. His family and my family were from the same town. They all went to the same schools. In a small town, everybody knows everybody. I assumed he already knew my family and wanted to see if I would be honest with him or if I would try to sugarcoat things and even lie. Any good parent wants to make sure their child is spending time with a good, honest person, right?

I thought to myself that I needed to tell it like it is—I needed to be honest. What I knew is that Eminem and Reba described people like me, how I grew up, as "trash." So with that understanding, I replied to Phil, and for everyone at the table to hear, "Well, I guess you could say that my family is white trash. I'm not really sure how else to describe us, but that is…"

And before I could finish, Phil had taken his napkin from his lap, swallowed his bite, wiped his mouth, and said, "Not here."

Everyone stopped eating and looked up. Silence. I could immediately tell something was wrong, although I did not understand what had happened.

With a stern, elevated voice, as if an enemy was in the room, he said, "In this house, we believe that every person is valuable, none better than the other. I will not let you come in my home, in front of my children and my wife, and use language like that. It is demeaning, disrespectful, and absolutely incorrect. Never again. Do you understand me, Alyson?"

I shook my head "yes," holding back tears. I was incredibly embarrassed and heartbroken. In a matter of seconds, I had shattered any possibility that the future with Joe I was already dreaming of could be a reality.

Phil went back to eating and everyone tried to move the conversation forward to alleviate the tension. I hardly spoke a word. I couldn't or else tears would flow.

After dinner was finished and everyone was carrying their dishes to the sink, I was ready to begin helping clean everything up. This was probably the last time I'd be in this house, so it was the least I could do. But Phil had other plans.

"Alyson, come into the living room with me," Phil said. I had no idea where this was about to go.

Phil directed me to sit down on the couch. He sat in the chair across from me. I can't remember exactly every word he said after that, but I remember the sentiment being that he did not intend to embarrass or hurt me. However, his job as the leader of the house is to protect his family, and my comment would likely have been extremely hurtful to the people I was talking about. And frankly, he said, it was absolutely incorrect; there is no such thing as human trash.

All of this was shocking to me.

First, I now clearly see just how immature, ignorant, and incorrect that 15-year-old girl was. I am so deeply embarrassed that I even thought that notion was okay to think, let alone say out loud to other people.

Second, while he was talking to me in the living room, I remember clearly thinking that this is what a man, a husband, a father should do. They should protect their people. They should stand up for what is right. They should fight anybody who would bring harm to their people. Far more often than not, I have learned what a man should be based off what I experienced them doing wrong. I remember thinking that what he did at the table must be love.

Finally, I remember looking back, thinking about our conversation in the living room, and feeling like I could come back.

I couldn't believe that.

I messed up—big time—in front of everyone. He quickly stood up for his family. He also taught me. He forgave me. He gave me permission to move forward with an improved perspective. I am a better person because of that night.

What is even more interesting is that while that experience was over 18 years ago as of the writing of this book, it still hits me in the gut. And now, Joe and I have been married for over 13 years. Phil, without a doubt, fills the father role in my life. And can you believe that we are now in business together? Phil has my full trust, and this moment was pivotal in establishing that.

That night, Phil met a paramount need of mine.

I needed to see what taking care of one's family looks like. I knew firsthand what it didn't look like. The fact that he stood up for his family was love. The fact that he took time to have a compassionate conversation with me after a heart-wrenching interaction—that was love. Maybe not in the sense that he loved me personally then, but you could say that he loved people and he saw a teenager who maybe didn't know anything different and he wanted to help. Because his actions served my need, I deeply connected with him that night. If he would be honest there, I thought, he would be honest going forward. I would seek out his input and allow him to influence my decisions. Hands down, he is one of the largest influencers in my life, and it all started that night with a hard conversation and an unforgettable follow-up on his part. Infinite Influence was built in the debrief that night.

EXAMINE YOUR INTENT

In the pursuit of improving your personal relationships, make sure you're after their win as much as you are yours.

Phil didn't want his family to be hurt so he addressed a problem outright. And it was equally important to him that I wasn't hurt that night either. Infinite Influence seeks mutually beneficial outcomes.

ASSESS YOUR AWARENESS OF THEM

Sometimes people act in certain ways because they don't know how to act, or at least don't know a better way. Attempt to understand them so you can think like them. When you can think like them, your next right step becomes clearer.

Phil understood that I didn't know any better. That information guided how he moved next to achieve Infinite Influence.

REFINE YOUR ACTIONS

A one-size-fits-all approach does not work when it comes to building Infinite Influence.

Always work to understand what people need from you in order to move forward better. It's there that true, deep, and lasting connection happens.

NEVER STOP SERVING

Sometimes Infinite Influence is achieved in a single moment. Other times, it's the strategy that steers and solidifies a relationship over time.

"When you can think like them, your next right step becomes clearer.

For as long as I've known Phil, he has consistently showed up as someone who values everyone and wants to help people be better. The foundations for Infinite Influence were built that night at his house over a decade ago, and since then his influence on me has continued to grow.

With whom do you need to follow up or debrief?

It might just be the follow-up conversation that creates the deep, lasting connection necessary to positively impact their life in ways you cannot even imagine yet.

CAPITALIZE ON HARD CONVERSATIONS

Most people avoid confrontation.

However, confrontation can be an incredibly effective tool for building Infinite Influence.

My daughter came home from school one day with a packet of coloring pages she was working on and was excited to show me. As I sat silently and flipped through the pages, I felt like I was looking at something inappropriate for her. Willow broke the silence and asked why there were boys laughing in her class as they worked on coloring these pages in their free time. On these coloring pages were cartoon figures of boys and girls. In every picture where a full body was shown, I saw girls in short skirts with their stomachs and cleavage showing. With puberty right around the corner, I knew exactly why a little boy might snicker at these images. I carefully pointed out to my daughter that these pictures showed areas of girls' bodies that these boys might never have seen before and

"Confrontation can be an incredibly effective tool for building Infinite Influence.

because they were a little unsure or uncomfortable, they laughed. She nodded her head as if to say, *Oh, I see that now,* since we have talked with her about privacy and her body.

The heart of this book has nothing to do with the sexualization of cartoon characters, so I am not going to go there. You may see nothing wrong with those pages. Okay. However, for the purposes of this book, I had a paramount need to protect the innocence of my child.

I praised my daughter for her coloring skills and sent her outside to play with neighborhood friends. My husband arrived home just in time for dinner. I had spent the last hour cooking and stewing over the fact that someone was intentionally or unintentionally encroaching on my daughter's childhood innocence, and potentially others' in her class whose parents I know and love, too. Mama bear was coming out. If you know, you know.

All six of us in the family were sitting at the table, and I firmly told Joe I was going to go have my first ever conversation with a schoolteacher tomorrow that might not go well. When he asked why, I simply told him I was going to ask her why she selected coloring pages that included enhanced private areas. Maybe, just maybe there was something I had not thought of. Or worse, maybe the teacher and I were on completely different pages about what was appropriate or not and one of us was going to have to make some changes in order to successfully move forward. Willow sat at the table listening the whole time, soaking it in. Joe responded with his eyebrows raised and eyes wide open, asking me if we could please have this conversation in private later, Alyson?! Realizing that was probably the best idea, I agreed. During our conversation later that night, we decided that I would go talk with the teacher later in the week when my schedule was open.

The very next night at dinner, when we asked our kids about the best parts of their day, Joe and I were shocked to hear Willow's revelation that the best part of her day was being brave and talking with her teacher about those pictures. Our plan was for me to go talk with the teacher in a few days, but instead Willow had taken the initiative to do so herself. She shared that she was nervous to speak up because she did not want her teacher to be mad at her. However, she said her teacher was so very nice and let her help pick out all new pictures for everyone in the class to color. Joe and I sat in shock—for many reasons!

1. Our young daughter made the decision to be really brave and have a hard conversation with an adult, face to face!

2. The teacher did not respond defensively or in anger! In a world where people are quick to be defensive and retaliate, I was surprised and heartened by the teacher's empathetic response—and I silently wondered whether I would be getting a call from the principal the next day.

3. The teacher let my daughter have a voice in creating new packets for the class that my daughter believed to be more appropriate. She engaged her rather than exiling her.

The next day, I called the school on my lunch break to talk with the teacher. I was terrified we were about to open a huge can of worms and become famous in a small town. We wanted none of that! However, when I called the school to talk with the teacher, she wasn't available. I didn't want to leave a message, but the office secretary said she would tell the teacher I called.

Early the next morning, before school even started, my daughter's teacher sent me a text message. Thinking the worst, I started reading through the seven-paragraph text.

In just the first few words, I was pleasantly surprised. The teacher was extremely complimentary of my daughter, even calling her "wise." It's possible that Willow created a moment in which she achieved Infinite Influence with her teacher by stepping out and speaking up. The teacher went on the explain that her intention was not to influence young minds in a sexual way. She thanked us for opening her eyes as she is also a parent and grandparent.

I felt so many emotions. Relieved that she was not angry or defensive or trying to push anything on the kids. Proud that she described my daughter as wise. Thankful that she was incredibly kind to her. Imagine if that would not have been the case! Imagine if my daughter had a life story where she spoke up for what she thought was right and she was met with anger, disappointment, and public embarrassment. That could have destroyed her confidence forever! Instead, my daughter's story is one in which she spoke up to leadership and was welcomed and invited to be part of positive change. That could improve her confidence for a lifetime!

What is even better is that a year later, Willow was getting out of the car at the pickup line and her old teacher was there. That teacher is there every morning. And every morning since that day, the teacher seems to make it a point to emphatically wave "hello" to me. Even better, Willow said this morning that hands down her favorite teacher ever is that very teacher. Because those hard conversations—between Willow and the teacher, and between the teacher and me—were handled in a way where everyone's needs were served (the need for transparency, change, encouragement in the moment and long afterward), a deep connection was built, and I have no doubt that Infinite Influence was achieved. I can say that with complete assurance on my part! I have a need for my daughter to be engaged, encouraged, and empowered. Because that teacher was open to critical feedback and met my daughter with kindness, compassion, and built her up, I would welcome the opportunity to listen, help, or support her anytime!

The next time someone comes to you with difficult feedback, view it as an opportunity for you to build Infinite Influence with them. As much as Infinite Influence can be built intentionally, through the application of specific steps, it can also be cultivated— and sometimes even more impactfully—in those unplanned moments, the ones in which a window is opened momentarily into someone's paramount need and you take the time to notice and respond purposefully to it. When your goal is always a mutually beneficial outcome, when you seek above all else to meet the needs of people, Infinite Influence can be achieved.

With whom do you need to have a hard conversation that you have been avoiding?

That conversation might just be the moment in which your Infinite Influence begins. You simply need to uncover and serve the specific, unique need of the other person first.

"When your goal is always a mutually beneficial outcome, when you seek above all else to meet the needs of people, Infinite Influence can be achieved.

The single greatest pursuit in this life is to positively impact the people around us. In order to do that well, you must seek to understand, serve to connect, influence for good, and never give up.

It is my most sincere hope that you pursue Infinite Influence in every single personal and professional relationship you have so that all your work will result in a more meaningful existence for you and those most important to you, both now and for generations to come.

I'm wishing you huge success!

All my love,
Alyson

MEET
ALYSON VAN HOOSER

Leadership Authority

**Leadership Consultant, Trainer, & Keynote Speaker,
Co-Owner of Van Hooser Associates, Inc.**

**Author of *Infinite Influence* & *Level Up*
& Inspirational Speaker on Leadership & Success**

ALYSON is on a sold-out mission to help leaders succeed in the complex, post-pandemic workforce! Alyson knows the pressure and responsibility of breaking through big obstacles to achieve great results — both personally and professionally.

As a trusted resource for managing, leading, and influencing people of all demographics and professional backgrounds, Alyson's management experience with Walmart, her leadership experience in the banking and insurance industry, and elected city council member – all by the age of 30 — equip her to relate authentically with the challenges leaders are facing. She deeply understands the price of admission to leadership and the keys for leveling up — now she guides leaders to achieve even greater results!

Alyson grew up in poverty and was abandoned by both of her parents as a child. These tough beginnings taught Alyson the radical power of an ownership mindset—one that transforms the trajectory of your life and helps you achieve audacious goals. Although, her success has not been built by grit alone – it was and continues to be her intentional, effective strategies that fuel her and her audiences forward. Her results-obsessed inspiration guides people at all stages of their career to make practical changes that drive real life success!

With Alyson's personal and professional strategies for success in tow, her event keynote presentations and training programs with company leadership teams from C-Suite level to high potential employees prepare leaders and teams across the country to successfully work together. Alyson's audiences return to work both energized and equipped to transform the way they lead themselves and their team and earn unprecedented success.

Her down-to-earth style hits you in the heart, opens your mind, and pushes you forward!

Bring Alyson Van Hooser to Your Organization through Books, Keynotes, & Leadership Development Training

CONTACT ALYSON

hello@vanhooser.com

To order more copies of *Infinite Influence*

or

To get more information on Alyson's latest keynotes or corporate leadership development training, visit:

alysonvanhooser.com

CONNECT WITH ALYSON ON SOCIAL:

 https://www.linkedin.com/in/alysonvanhooser/